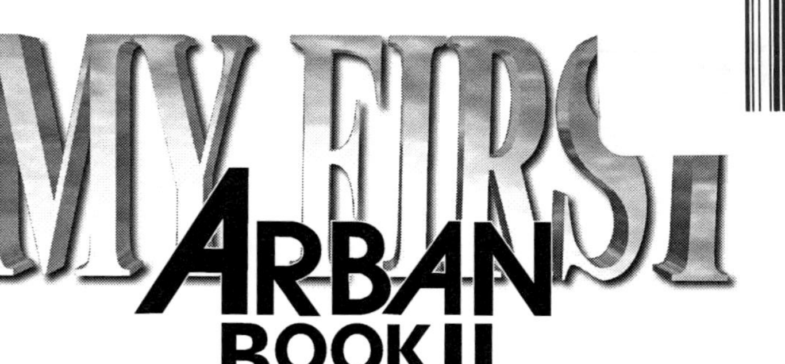

FOR THE DEVELOPING STUDENT

COMPILED AND EDITED
BY ROBERT E. FOSTER

THE CONTINUING INTRODUCTION TO ARBAN'S COMPLETE CONSERVATORY METHOD

Table of Contents

* The page numbers are references to Arban's *Complete Conservatory Method* (Carl Fischer Catalogue Number O21X).

CARL FISCHER®

Printed in the U. S. A.

WF78

ISBN 978-0-8258-6825-2

Preface

My First Arban, Book II is the logical next step following the use of the first book. This is a continuation of the introductory studies, technical exercises, and flexibility studies which are essential for the mastery of brass playing, and for which the *Complete Conservatory Method* is so well known.

Arban's *Complete Conservatory Method* is the most famous and most successful instrumental music instruction book ever written. It has been used successfully by more students and teachers than any other book in the history of brass instruments.

First published in 1864, the early editions of this book were printed with all instructions written in three languages, and the *Complete Conservatory Method* is still presented that way today. Now, over 100 years later, it is used all over the world. It is used anywhere and everywhere that people are serious about becoming great performers on brass instruments.

It is commonly referred to as the "Bible" for brass players. No book has ever been so universally accepted by the serious teachers and performers in a given area. This is the GREAT brass method!

How To Use This Book

In preparing *My First Arban Book II*, great care has been taken to preserve the original format and musical and educational objectives for which the *Complete Conservatory Method* is so well known. Consequently, many of the exercises and studies are exactly as they are in the original book, however, there are many areas where the studies started at a level of difficulty which made it unrealistic for many young players.

In these situations the keys, the rhythms, and the range of the exercises have been altered to provide introductory material which will enable the young student to prepare for a smoother, and much easier transition into the *Complete Conservatory Method.*

It is recommended that as the student moves into the more technical exercises, that they practice them slowly and accurately at first, being particularly careful to use correct playing habits and articulations before gradually increasing the tempo.

Remember, sit (or stand) correctly, hold your instrument correctly, breathe correctly, and do use a lot of air. Generally you need to establish the habit of using more air as you ascend, or play higher. Crescendo as you ascend, and diminuendo as you descend.

This book presents a "balanced diet" of daily practice or study routines. It is expected that the student (and teacher) will begin with the basic studies, with an assignment of basically one line of music in each different technical area.

For example, start with one line of Intervals, one line or exercise of Syncopation, one exercise of Rhythmic Studies (dotted 8ths and 16ths), Slurs, and a Scale study. This is a good starting place. Then the player should progress through each technical area, gradually moving into the more complex exercises and studies as he or she is able.

Enjoy your new musical adventure, and good luck!

–Robert E. Foster

Jean-Baptiste Arban

Jean-Baptiste Arban was born in Lyons, France, February 28, 1825. He entered the conservatory at an early age, and began studying the cornet. He became a professor of cornet at the conservatory in Paris in 1869, and began writing the exercises and musical studies which later became his famous method.

He was the most brilliant cornet player of his time, and he became very well known for his musicianship and for his excellence as a teacher, all of which have been perpetuated through his book.

Arban died in Paris on April 9, 1889, and is remembered today as the first great brass pedagogue, and as one of the greatest brass teachers who ever lived.

About the Editor

Robert E. Foster has a rich history of involvement in music going back over a half-century to his early band experiences in his father's school band in Texas soon after the end of World War II.

Following a successful professional performing career, (performing as a trumpet player with the Austin and the Houston Symphony Orchestras), and experience teaching in the Texas public schools, he joined the faculty at the University of Florida before becoming director of bands at the University of Kansas in 1971.

In addition to his work at the University, he maintains an active schedule as a conductor, clinician and adjudicator.

Fingering Chart for the B♭ Trumpet

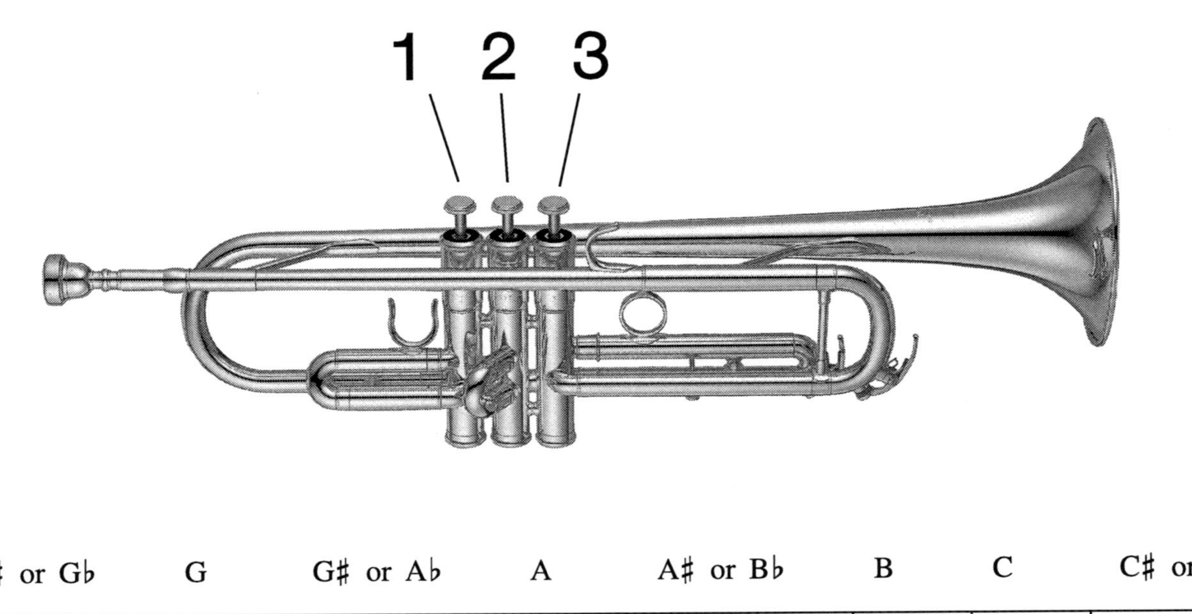

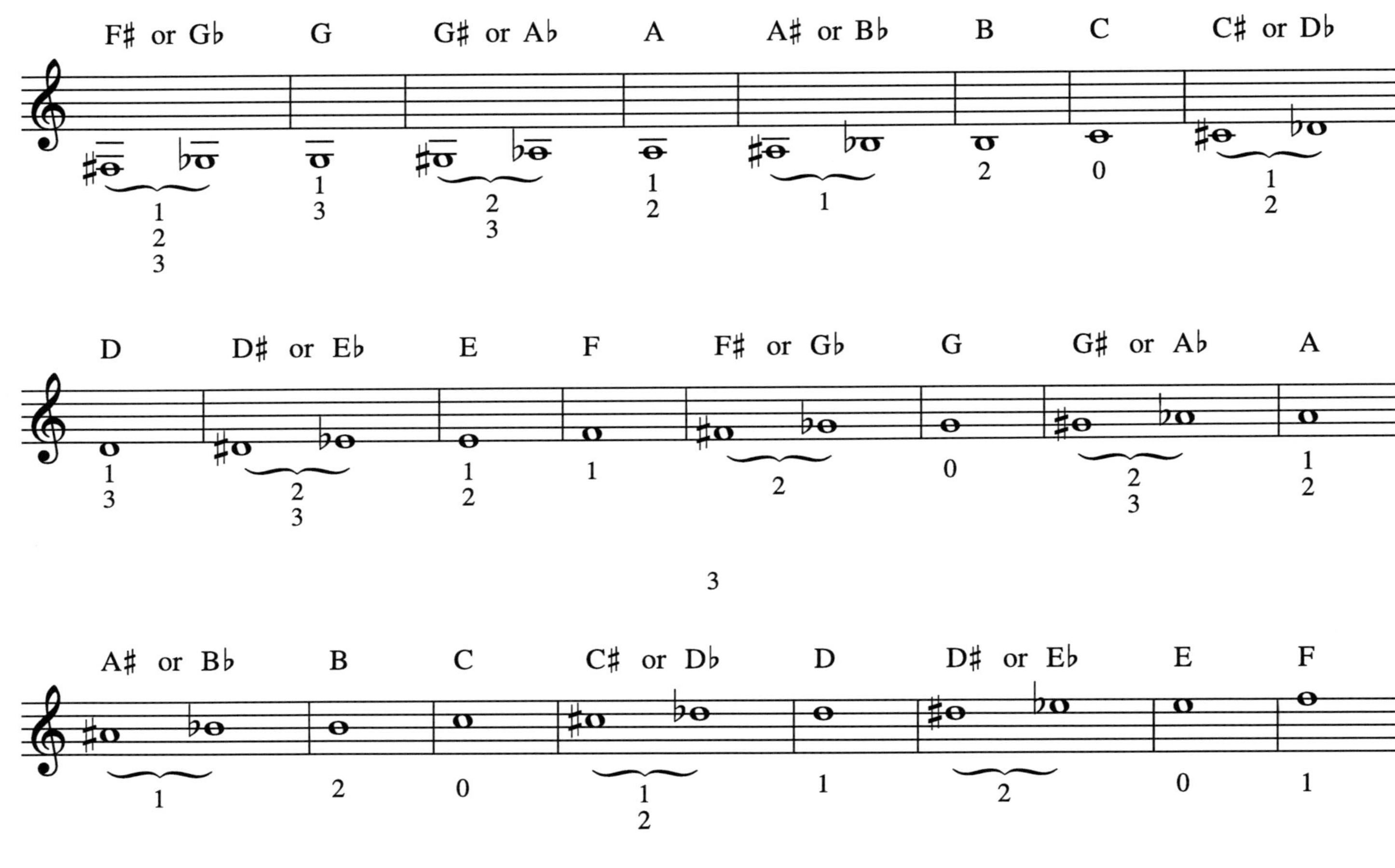

Remember that low C♯ and low D are always sharp. Always extend the third valve slide when playing low C♯ and D. Also, remember that the fourth line D and fourth space E♭ and E are flat partials in the harmonic series, and care must be taken to not let them be flat.

First Studies

correlates to page 6 in *Complete Conservatory Method*

① Key of C

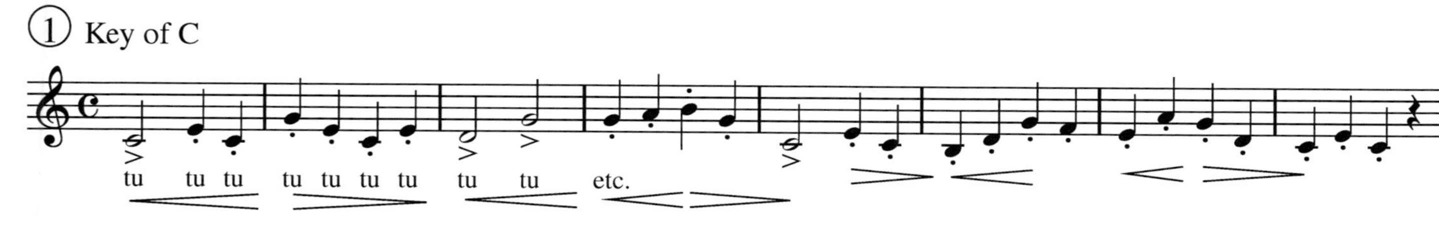

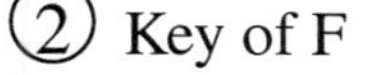

② Key of F

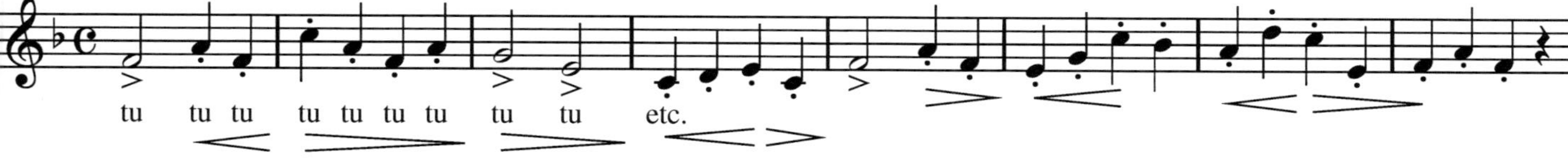

③ Key of G

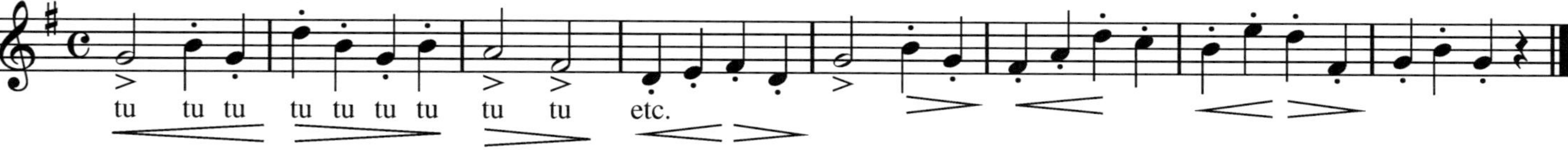

④ Key of B♭

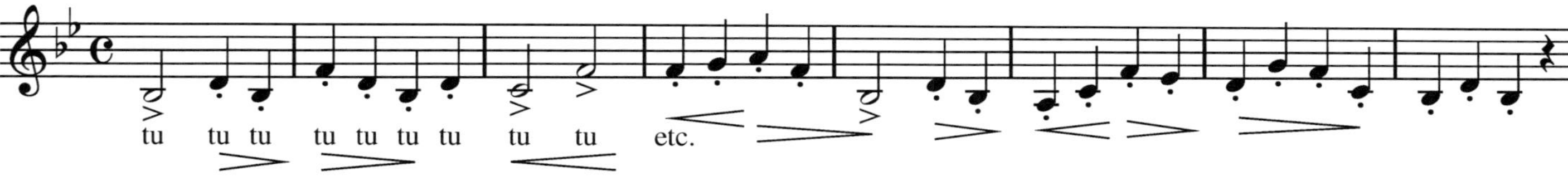

⑤ Key of E♭

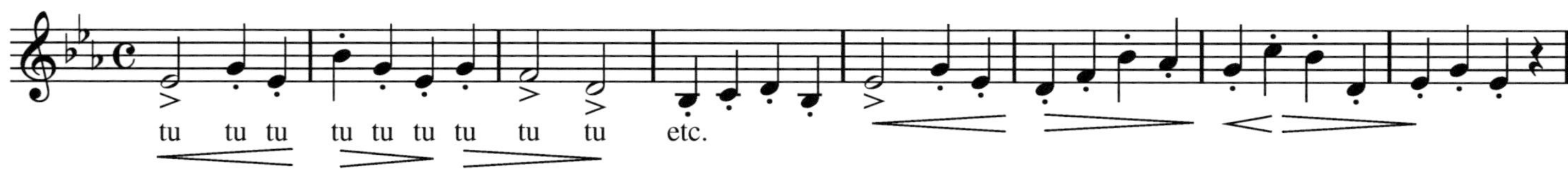

⑥ Key of F

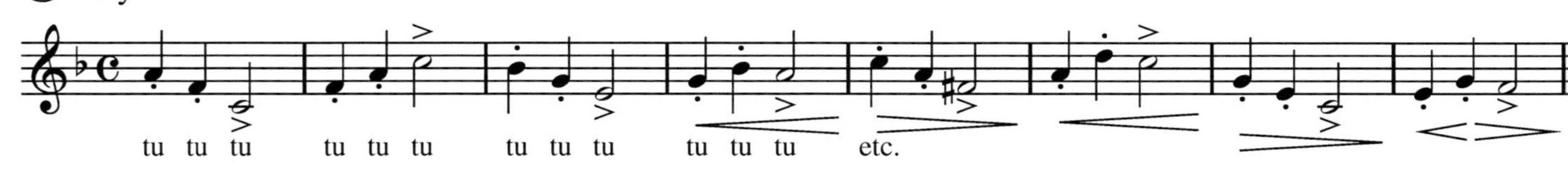

⑦ Key of G

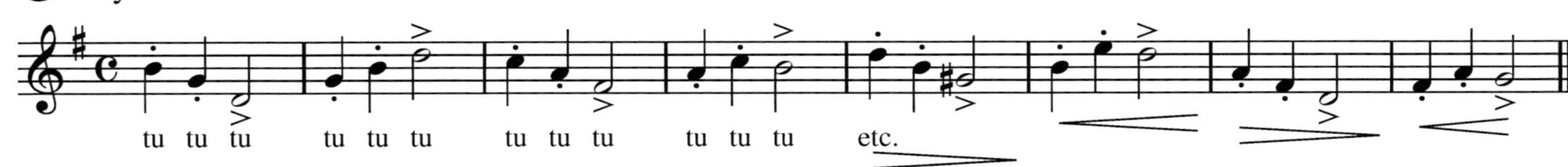

More First Studies

correlates to page 10 in *Complete Conservatory Method*

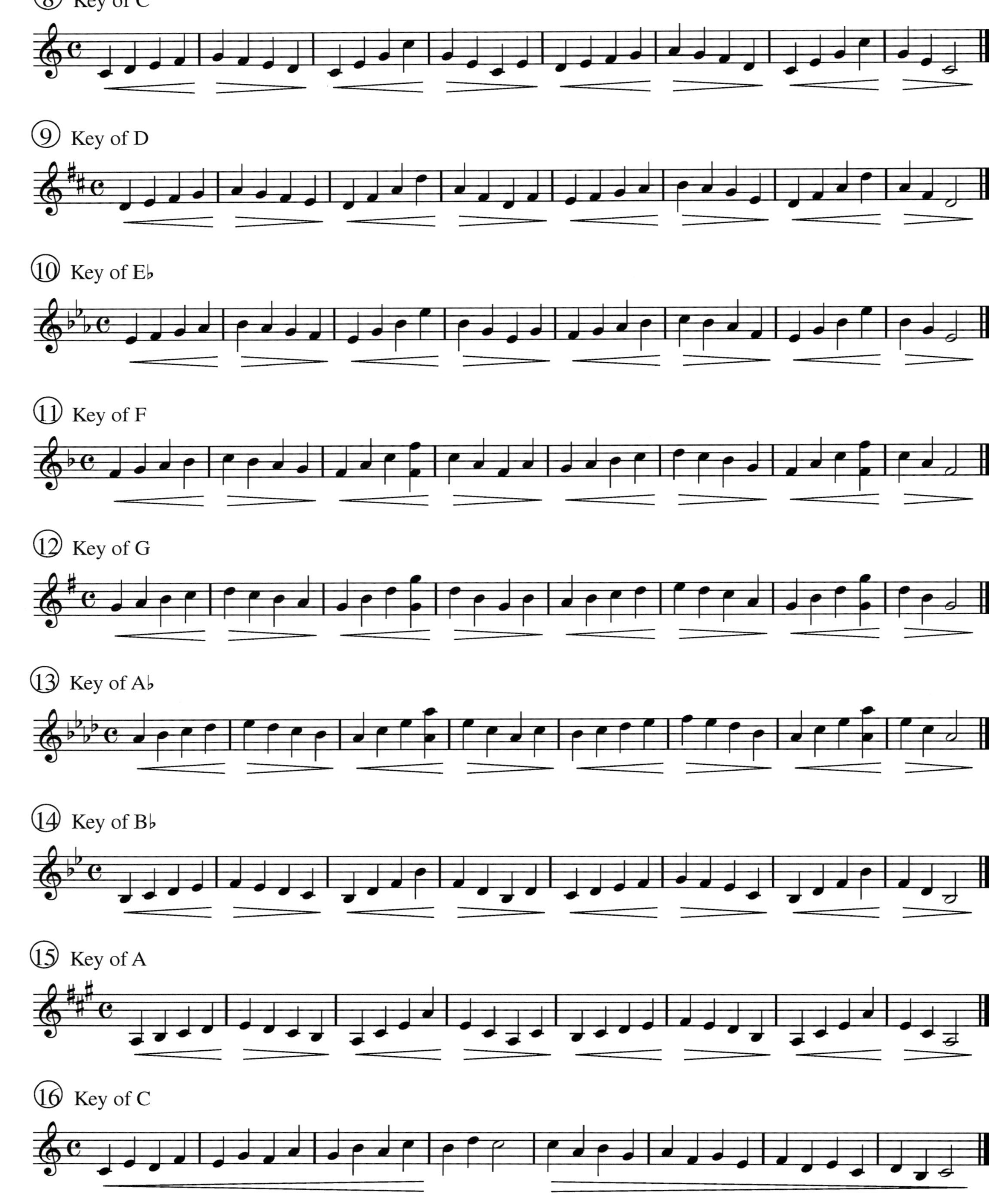

Syncopation

correlates to page 21 in *Complete Conservatory Method*

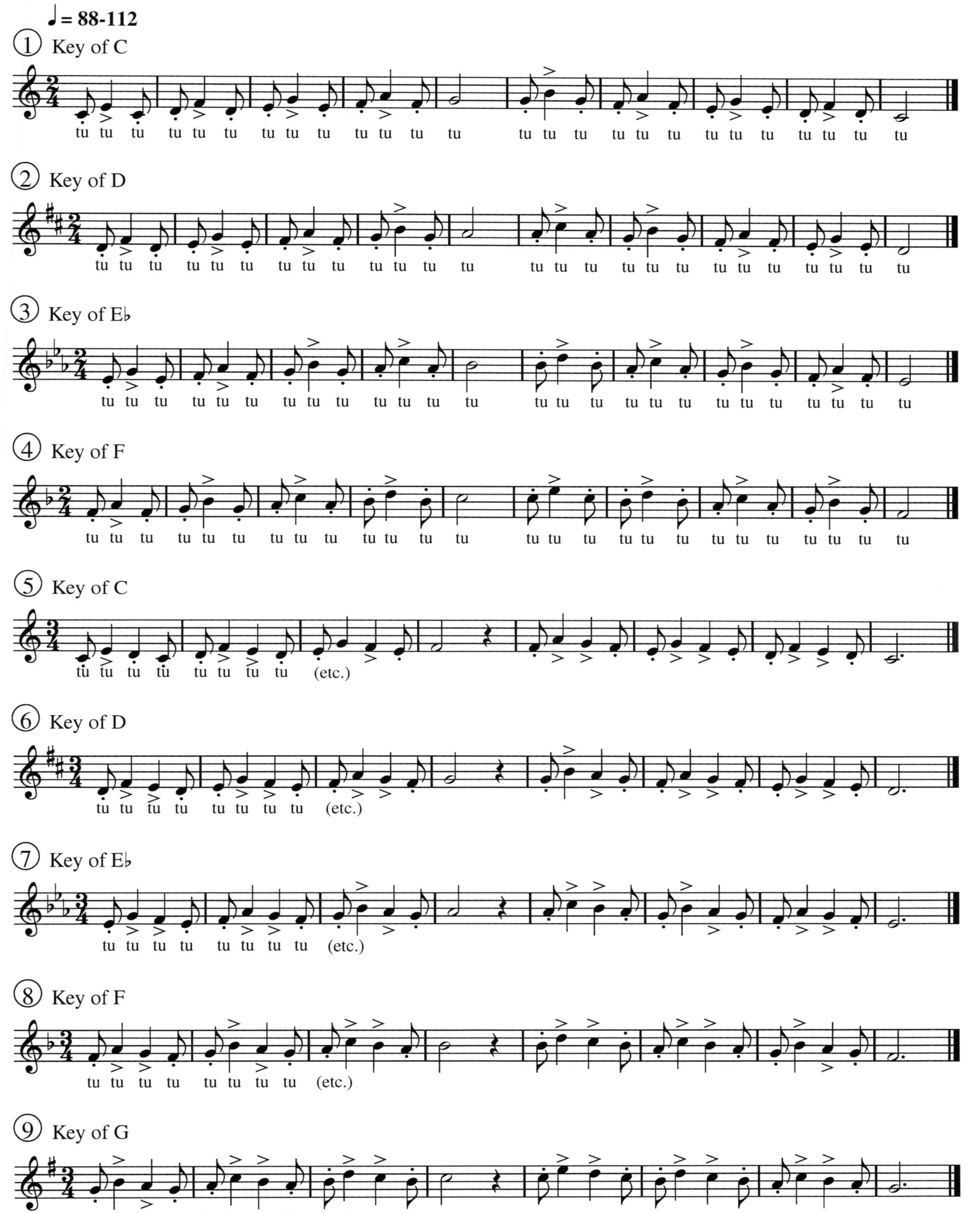

Dotted Eighths and Sixteenths

correlates to page 24 in *Complete Conservatory Method*

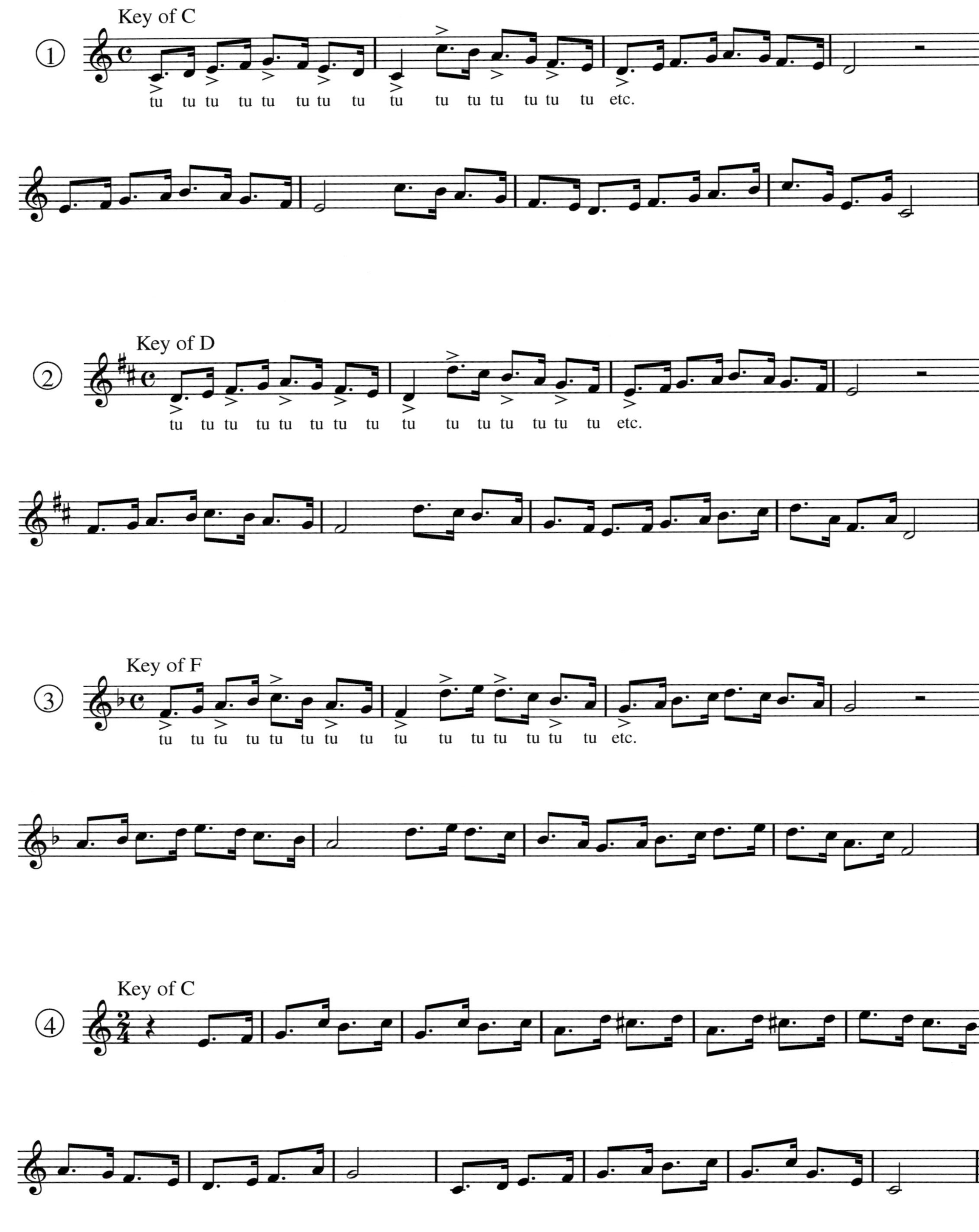

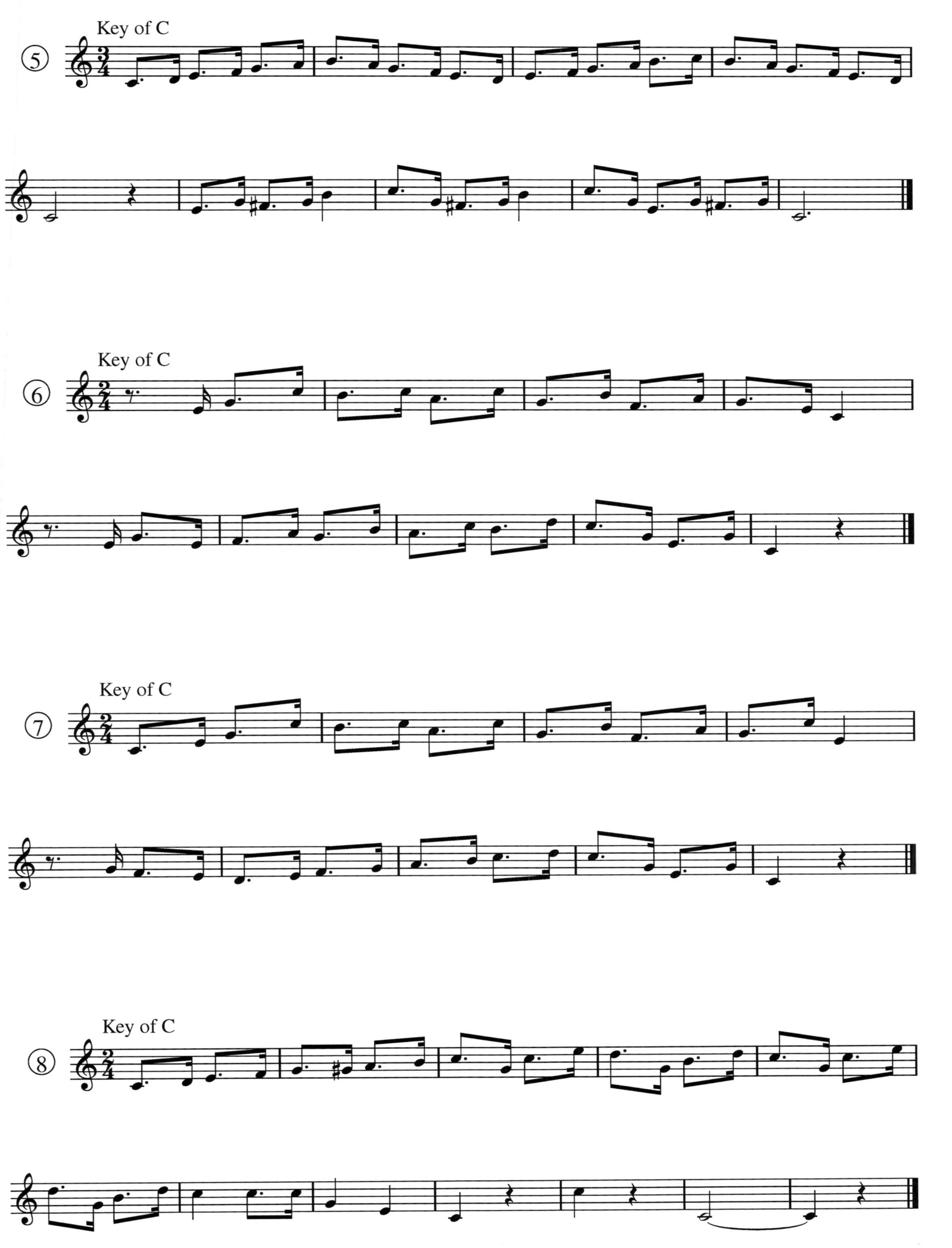
Key of C
5
Key of C
6
Key of C
7
Key of C
8

Rhythmic Figures ♪ and ♫

correlates to page 26 in *Complete Conservatory Method*

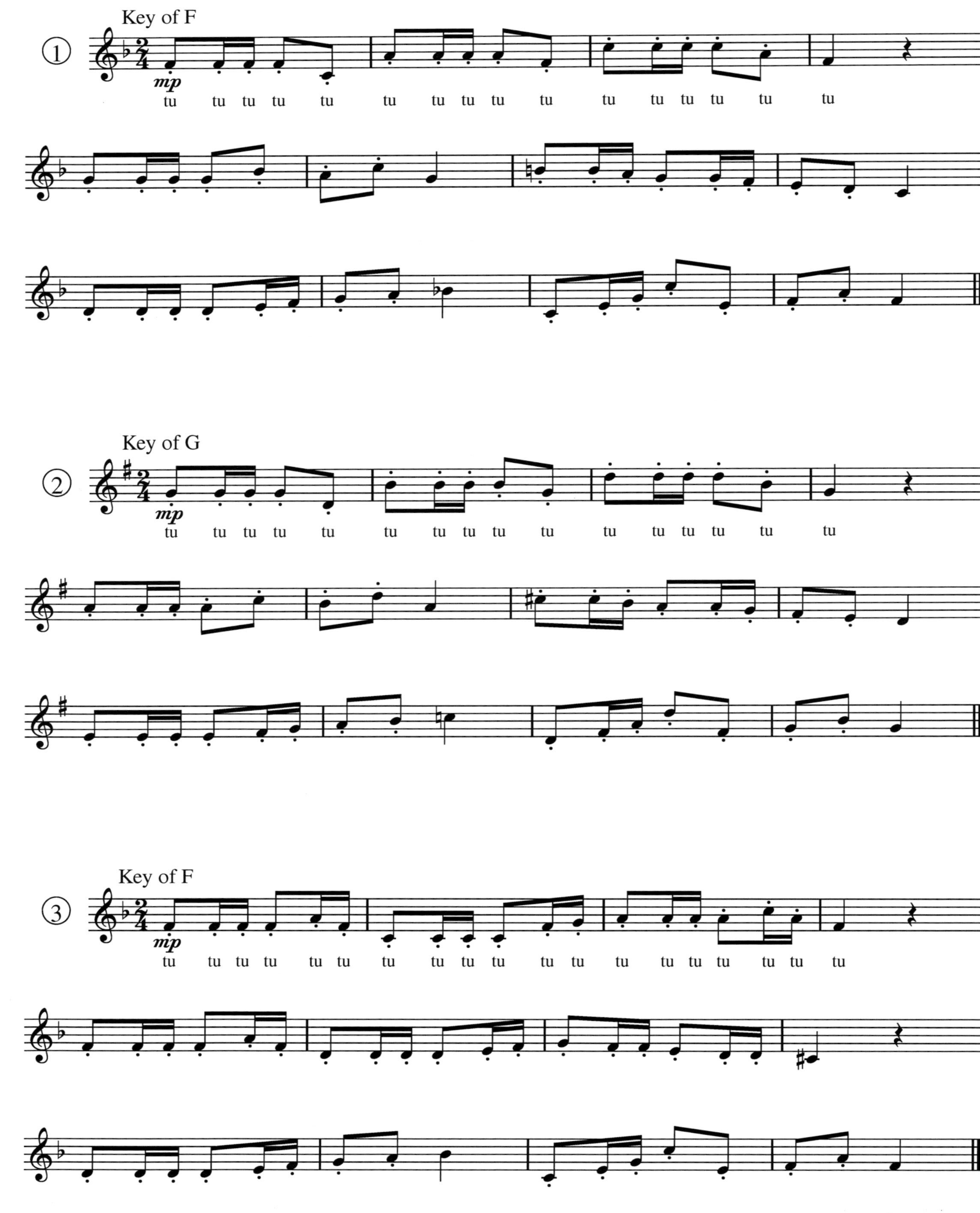

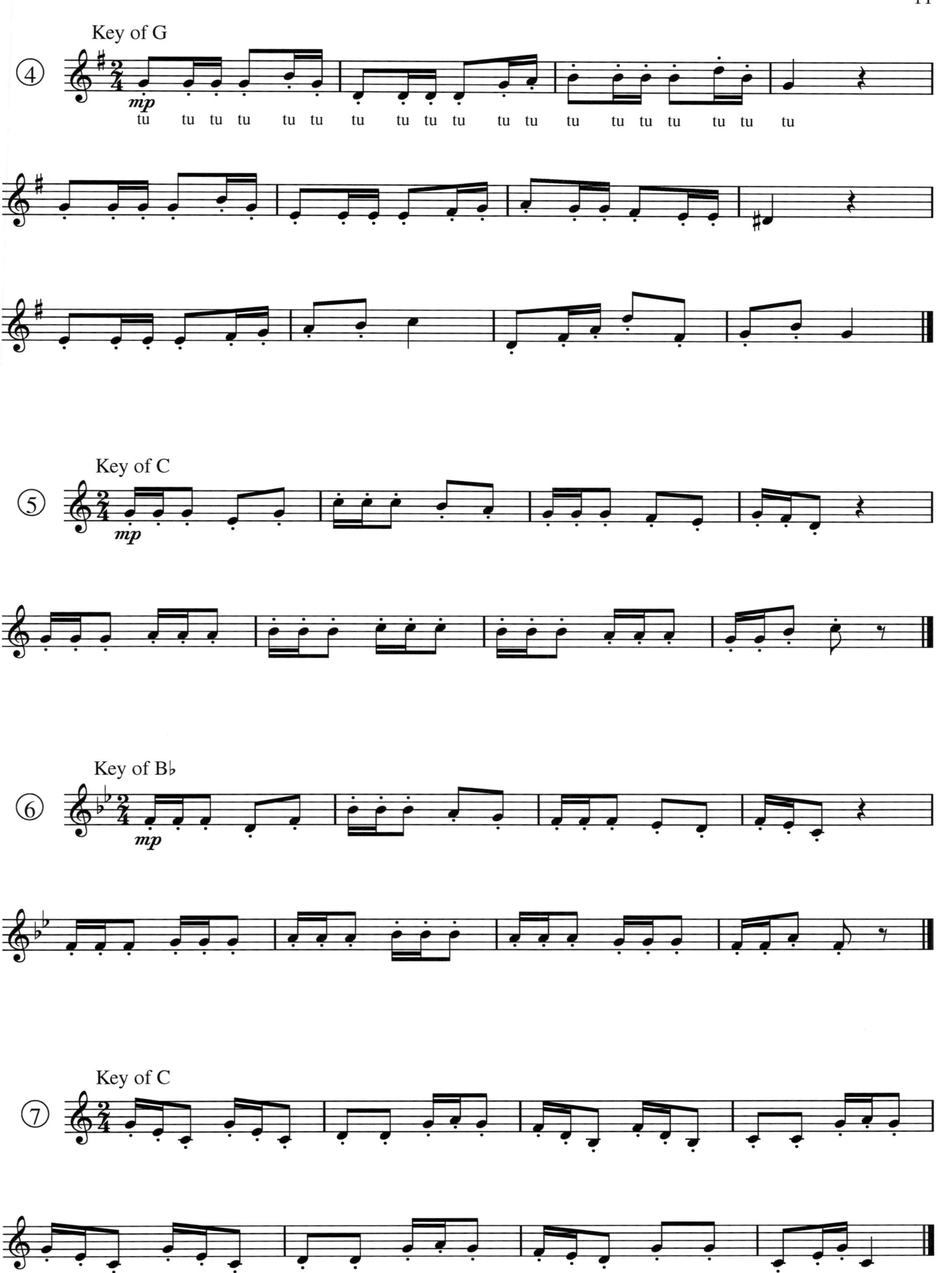
Key of G
4
mp
tu tu tu tu tu tu tu tu tu tu tu tu tu tu tu tu tu tu tu
Key of C
5
mp
Key of B♭
6
mp
Key of C
7

$\frac{6}{8}$ Meters

correlates to page 30 in *Complete Conservatory Method*

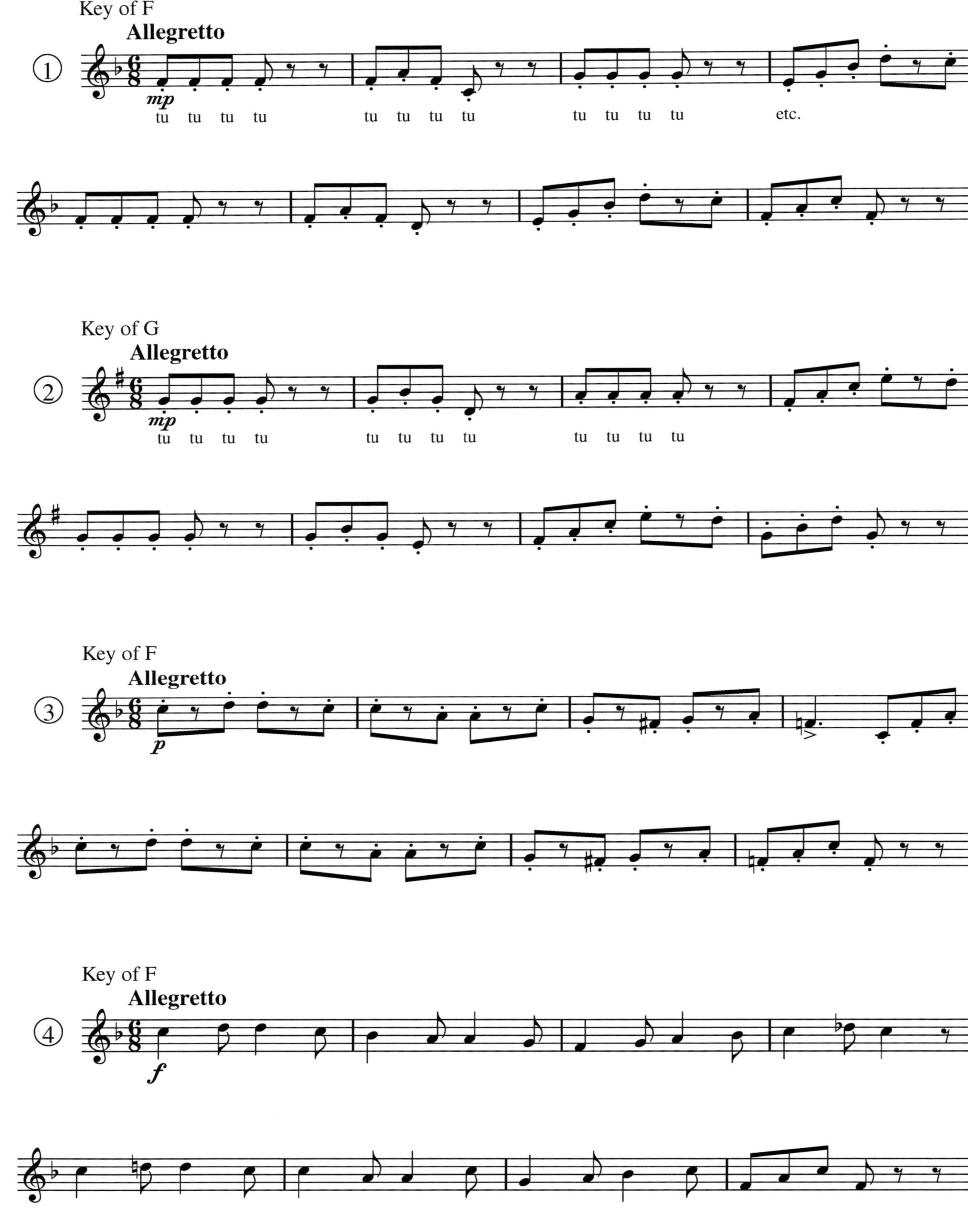

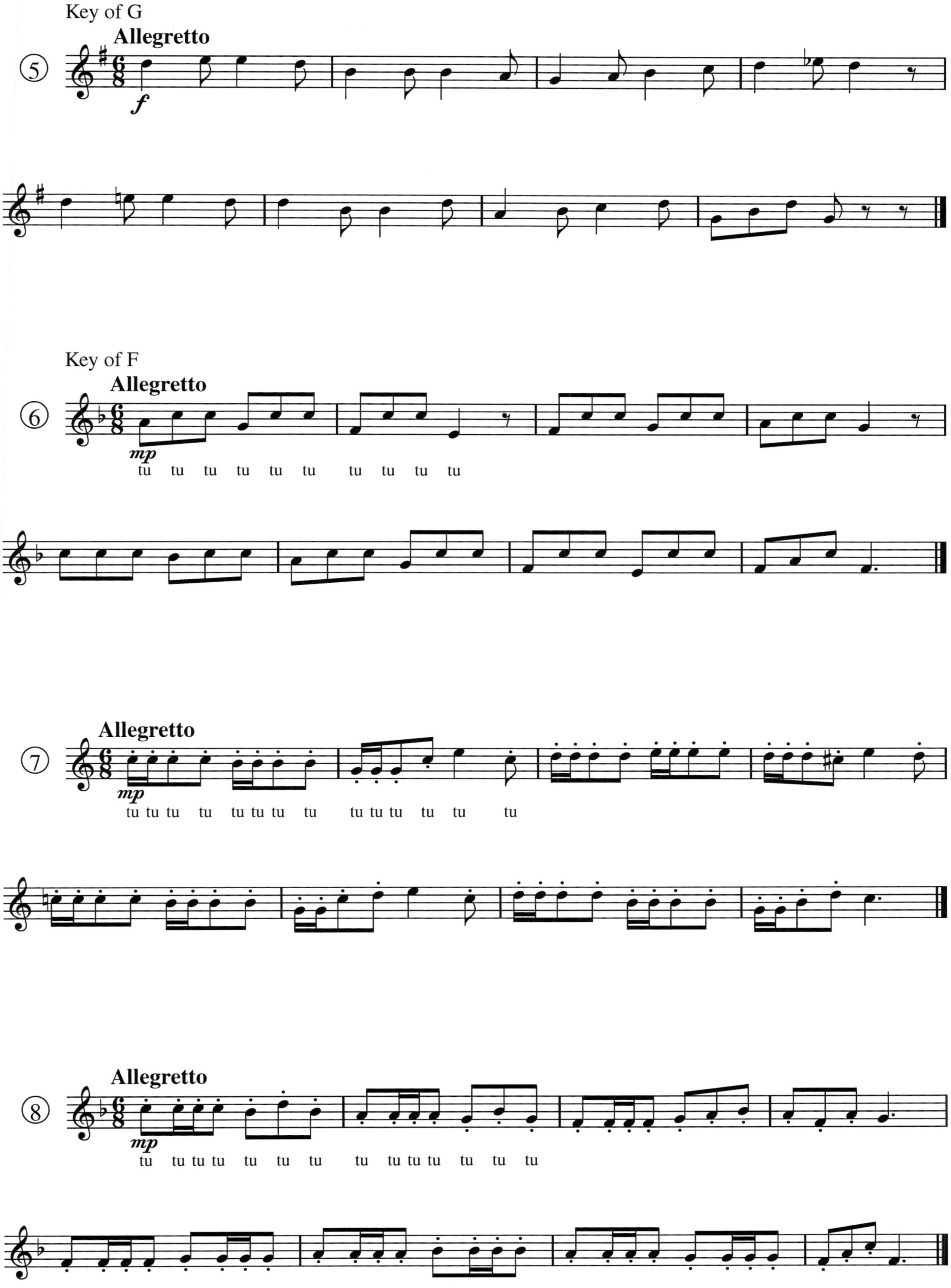

Key of G

Allegretto

5

f

Key of F

Allegretto

6

mp

tu tu tu tu tu tu tu tu tu tu

Allegretto

7

mp

tu tu tu tu tu tu tu tu tu tu tu tu tu tu

Allegretto

8

mp

tu tu tu tu tu tu tu tu tu tu tu tu tu tu

Slur Studies

correlates to page 37 in *Complete Conservatory Method*

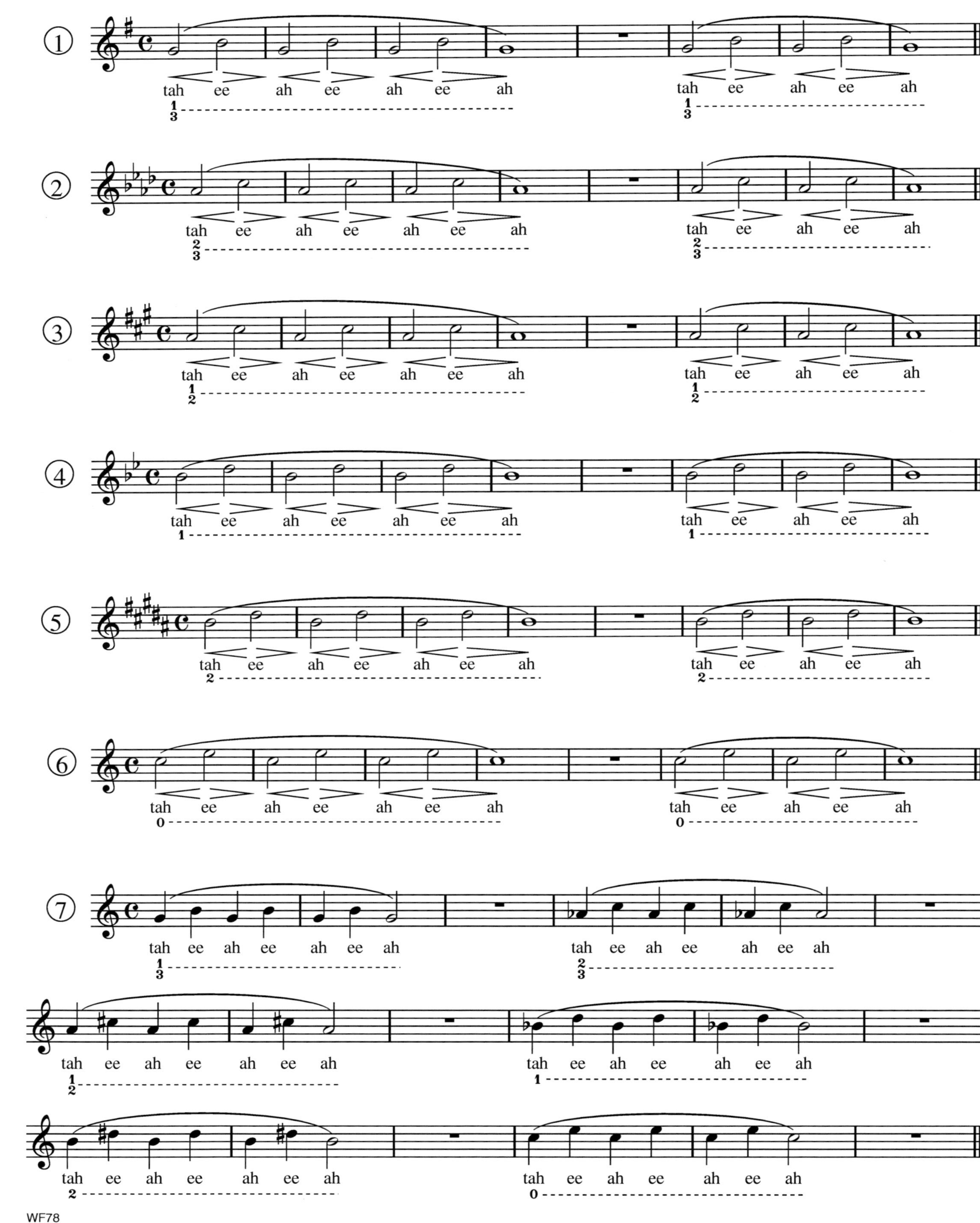

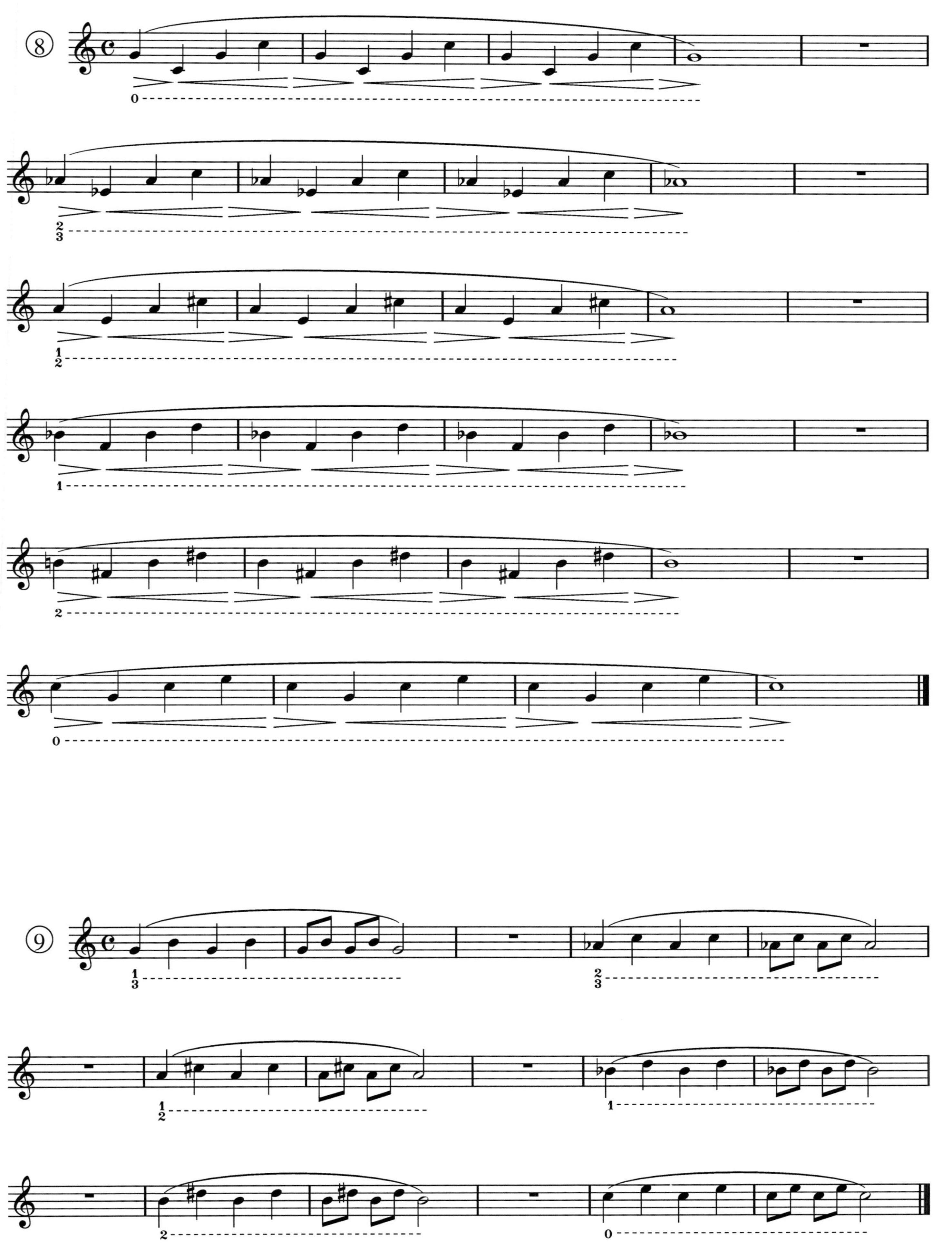
8
0
2
3
1
2
1
2
0
9
1
3
2
3
1
2
1
2
0

Major Scale Studies

correlates to page 62 in *Complete Conservatory Method*

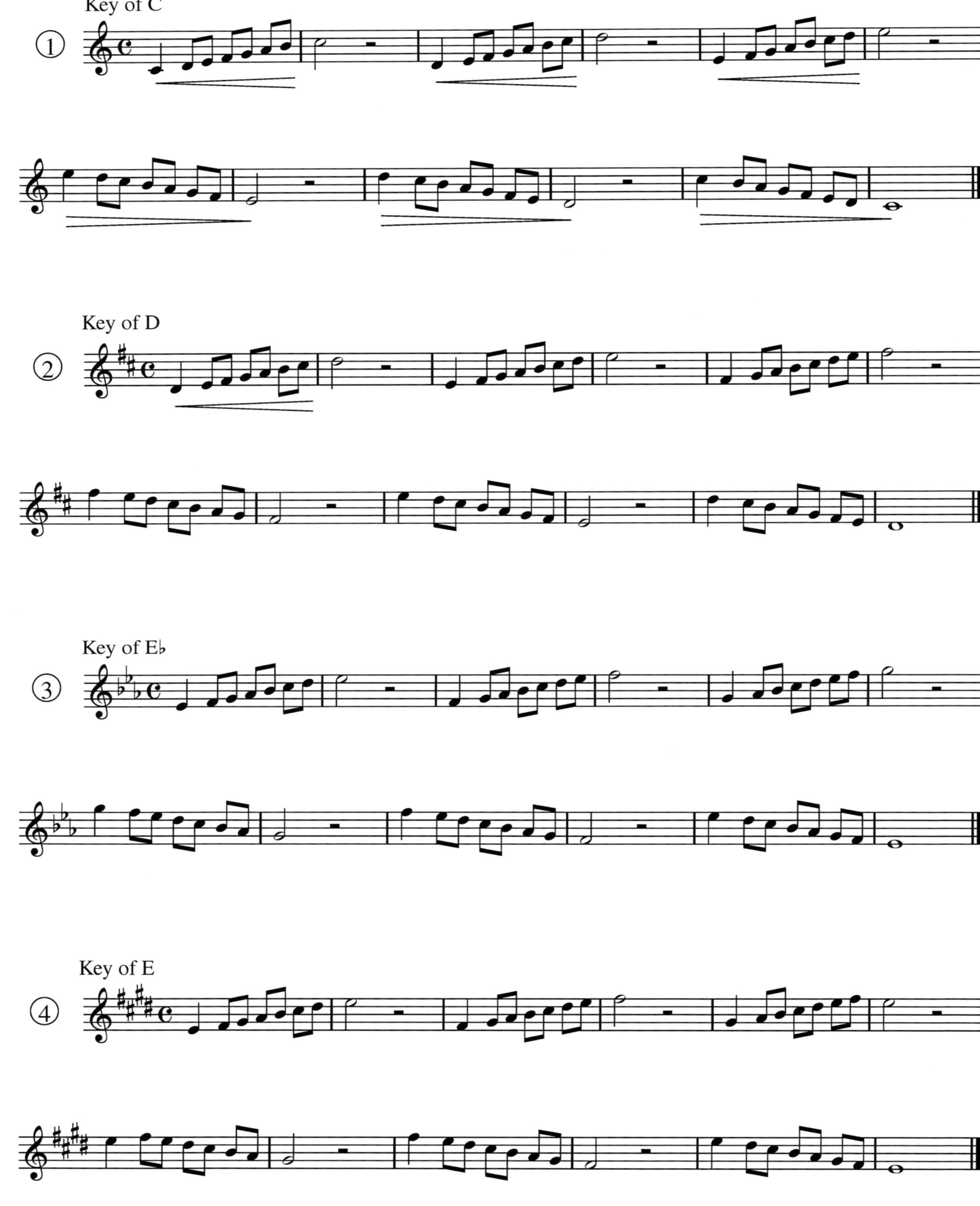

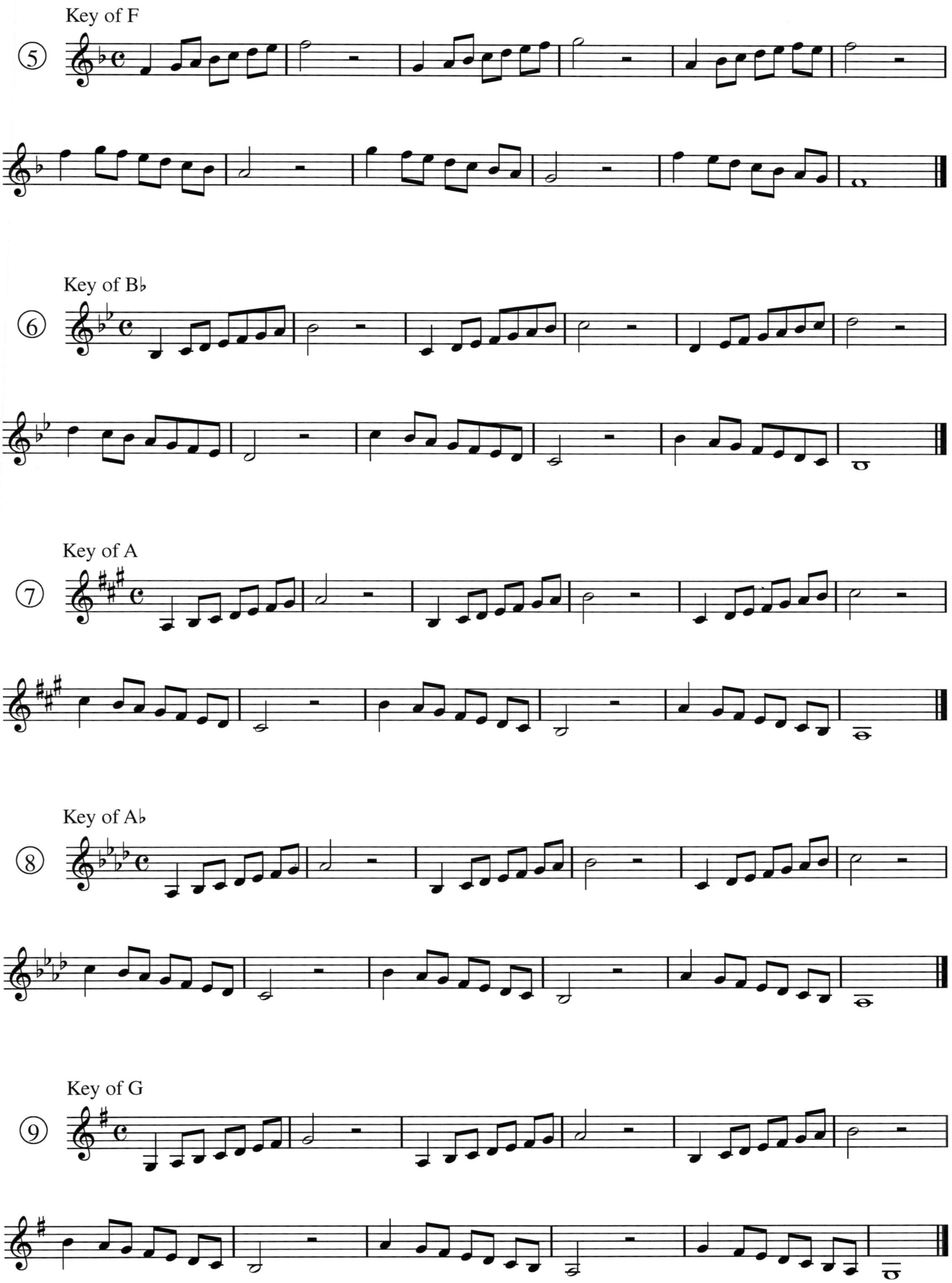

Key of F

5

Key of B♭

6

Key of A

7

Key of A♭

8

Key of G

9

More Major Scale Studies (1)

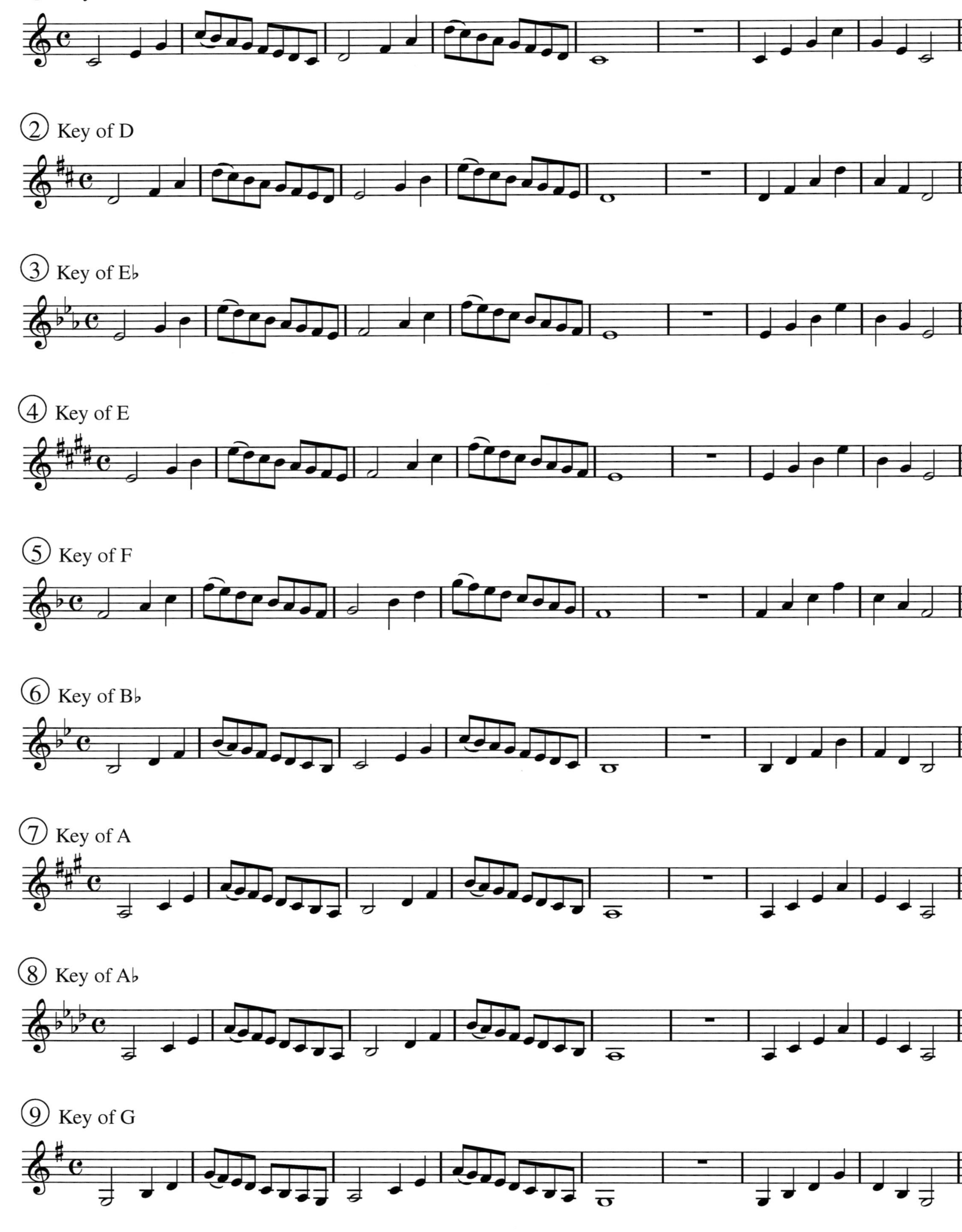

More Major Scale Studies (2)

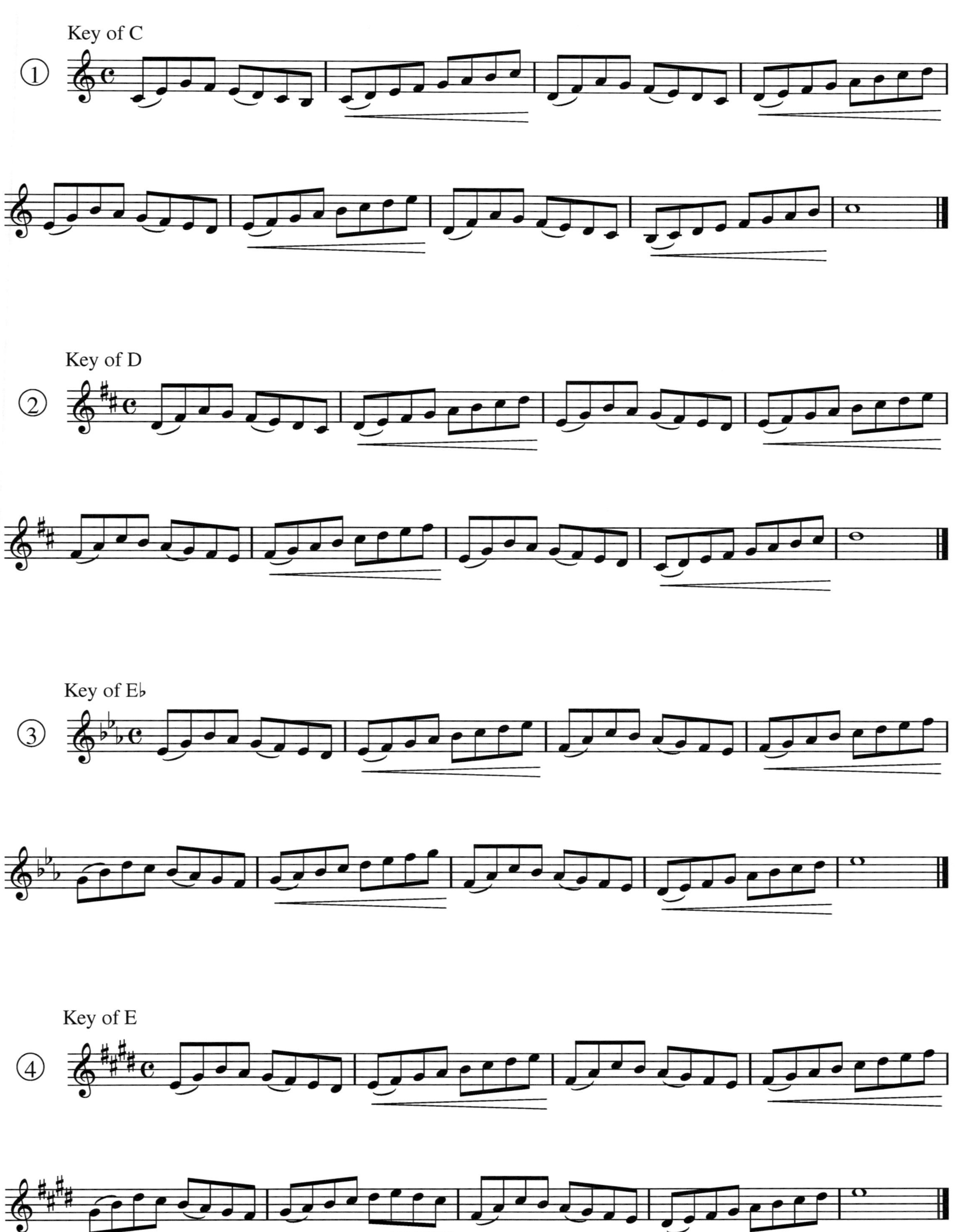

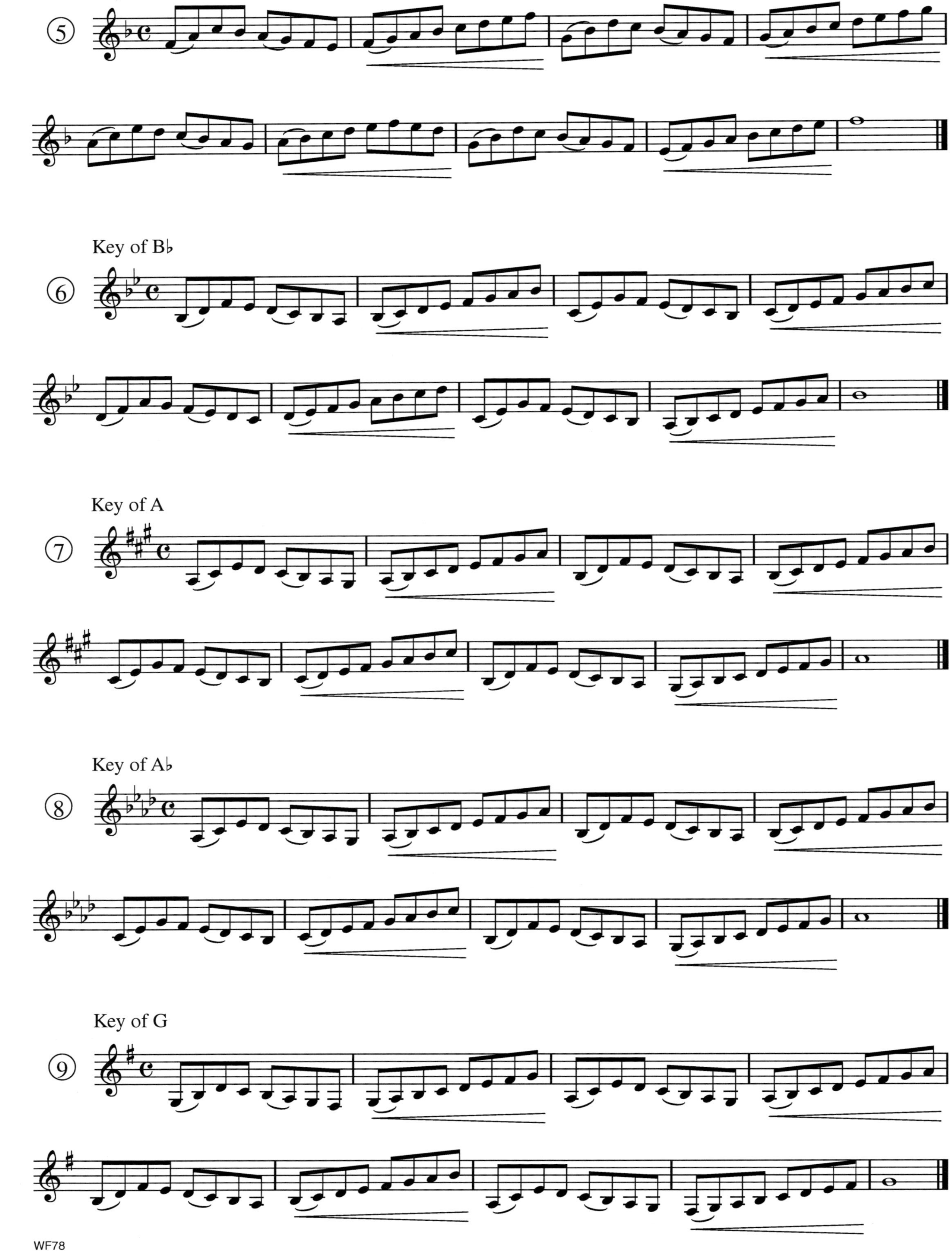
Key of F
5
Key of B♭
6
Key of A
7
Key of A♭
8
Key of G
9

More Major Scale Studies (3)

correlates to page 64 in *Complete Conservatory Method*

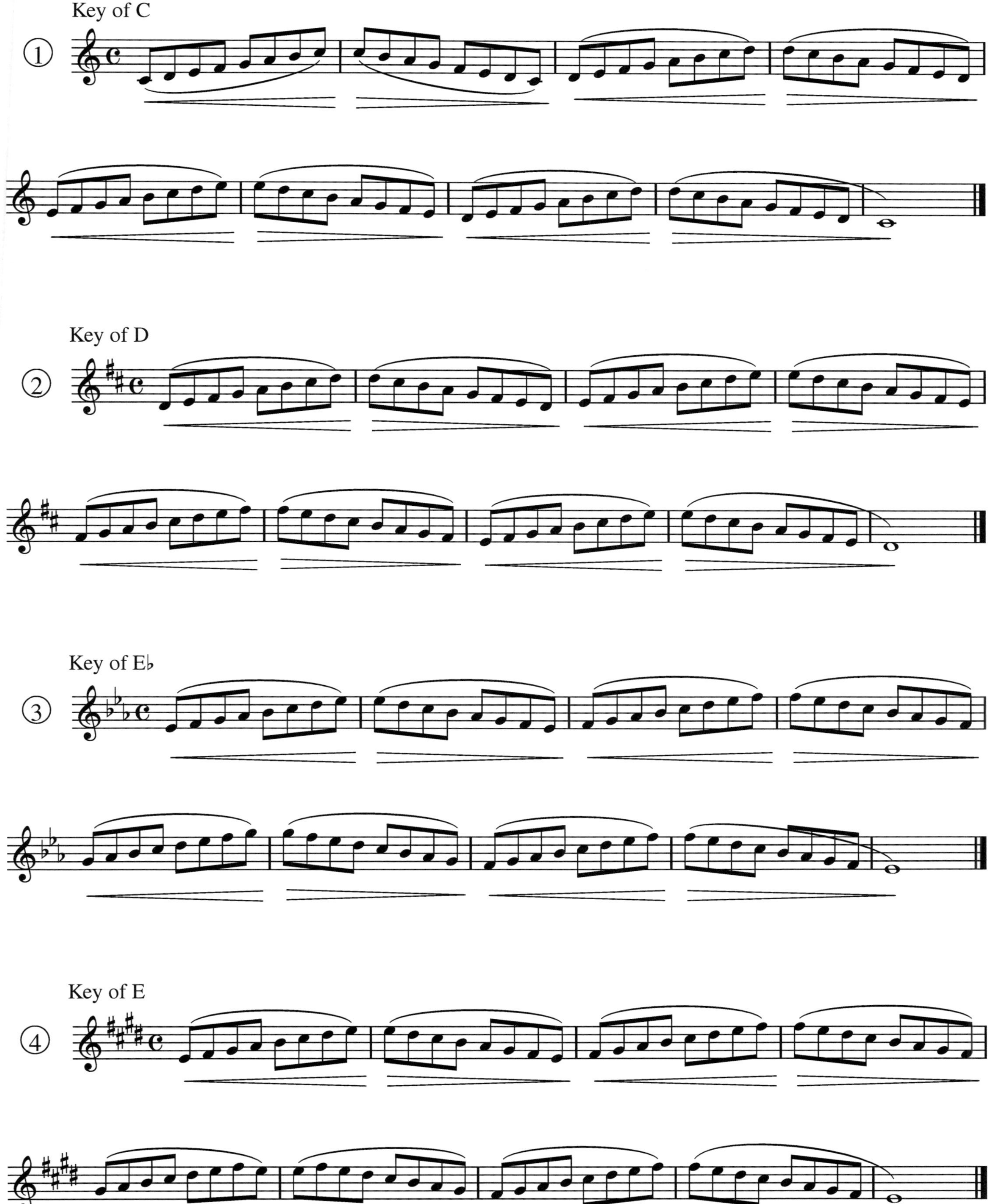

Key of F

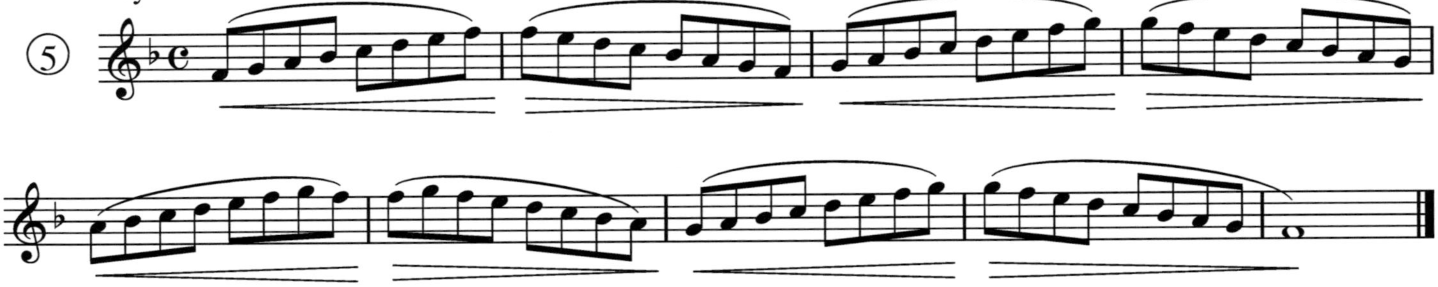

⑤

Key of B♭

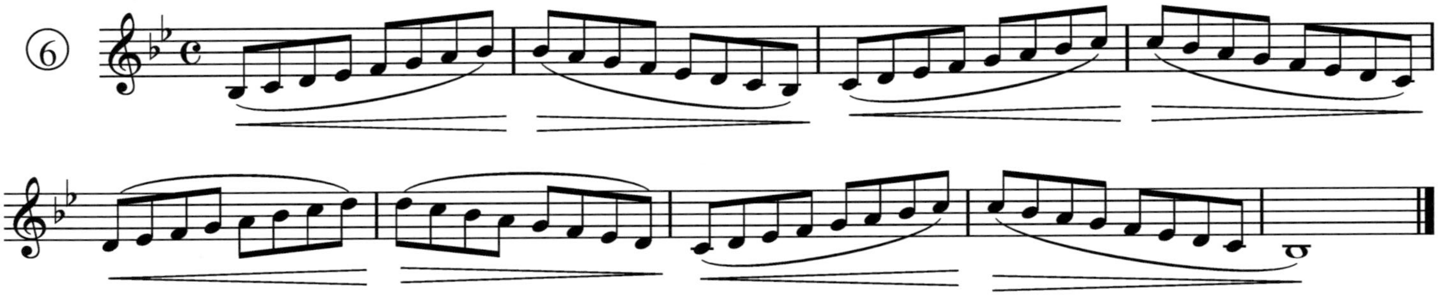

⑥

Key of A

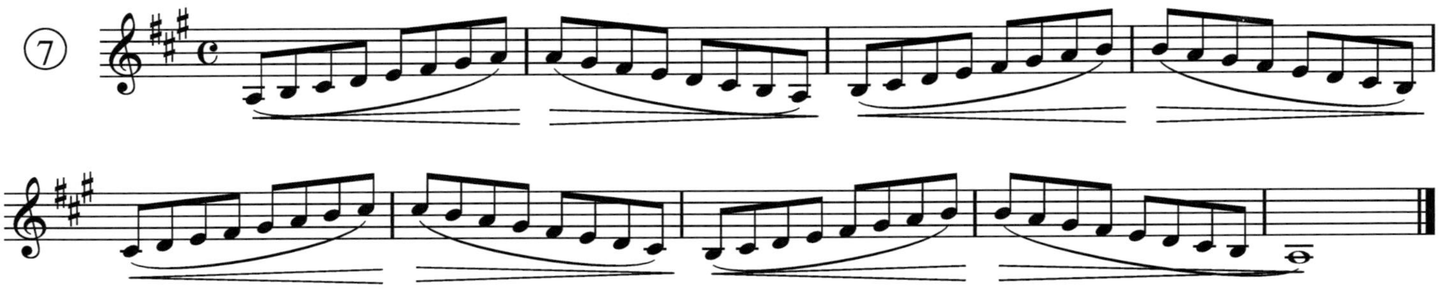

⑦

Key of A♭

⑧

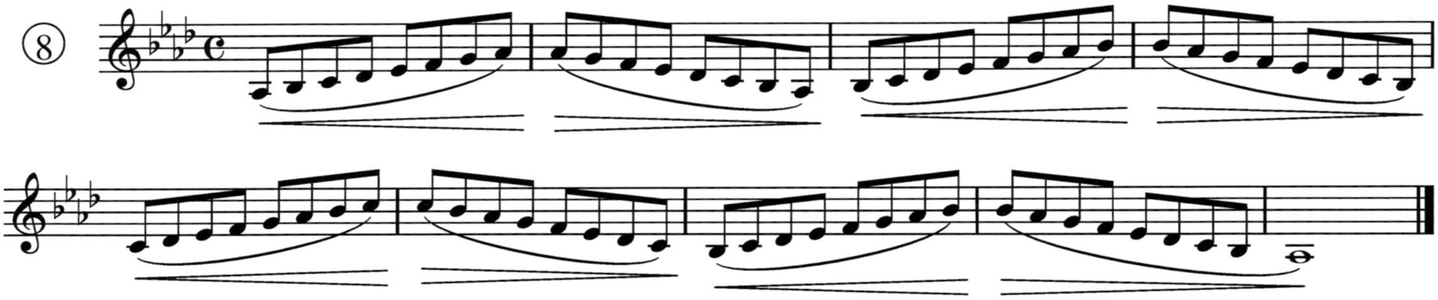

Key of G

⑨

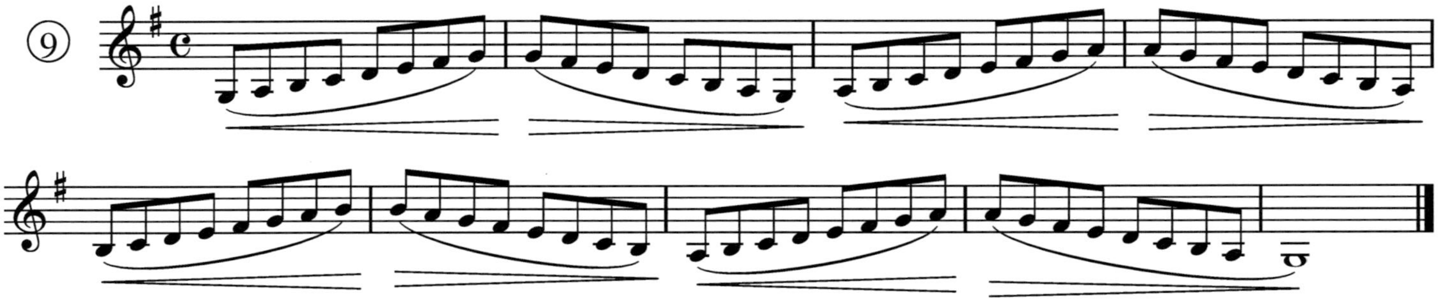

More Major Scale Studies (4)

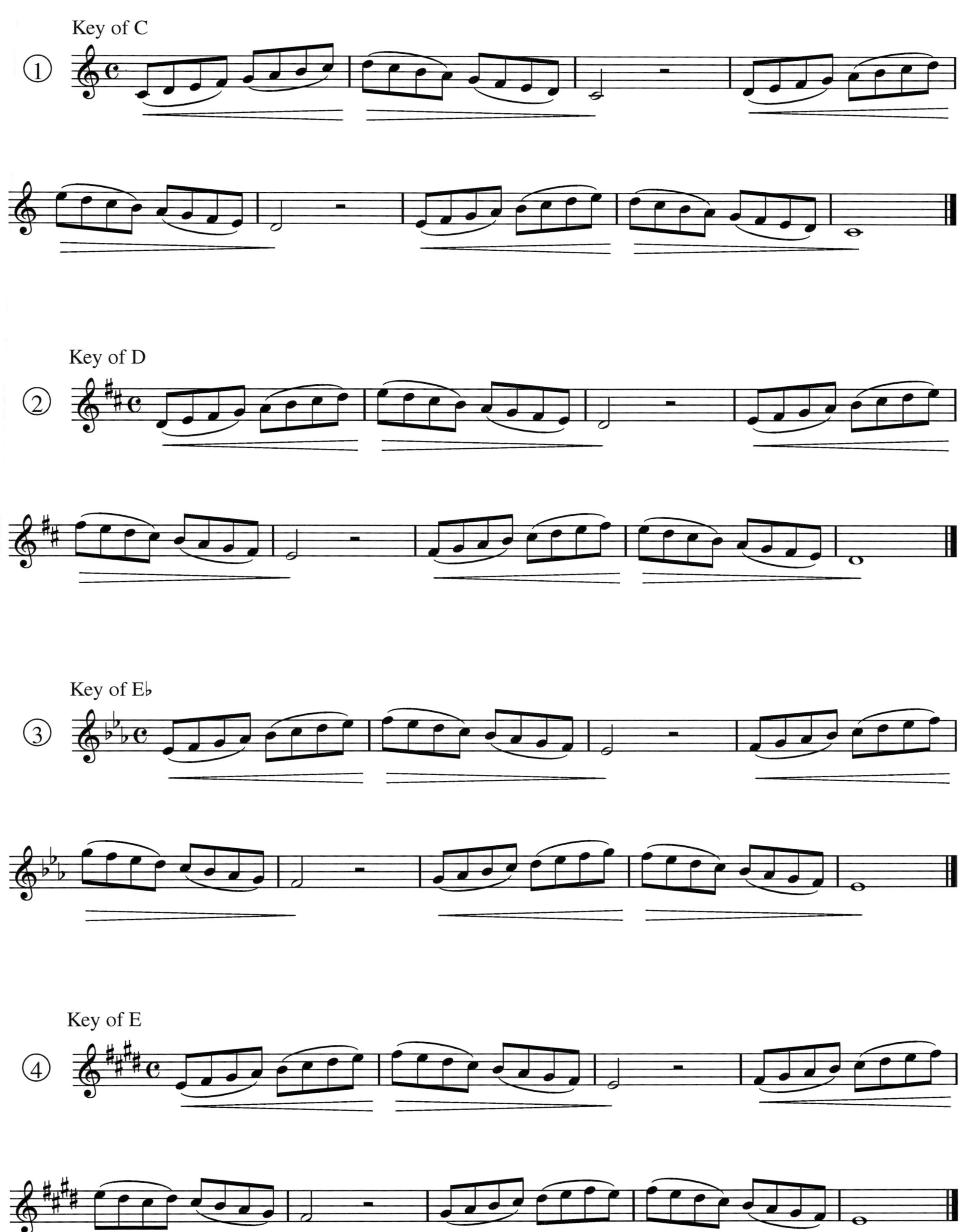

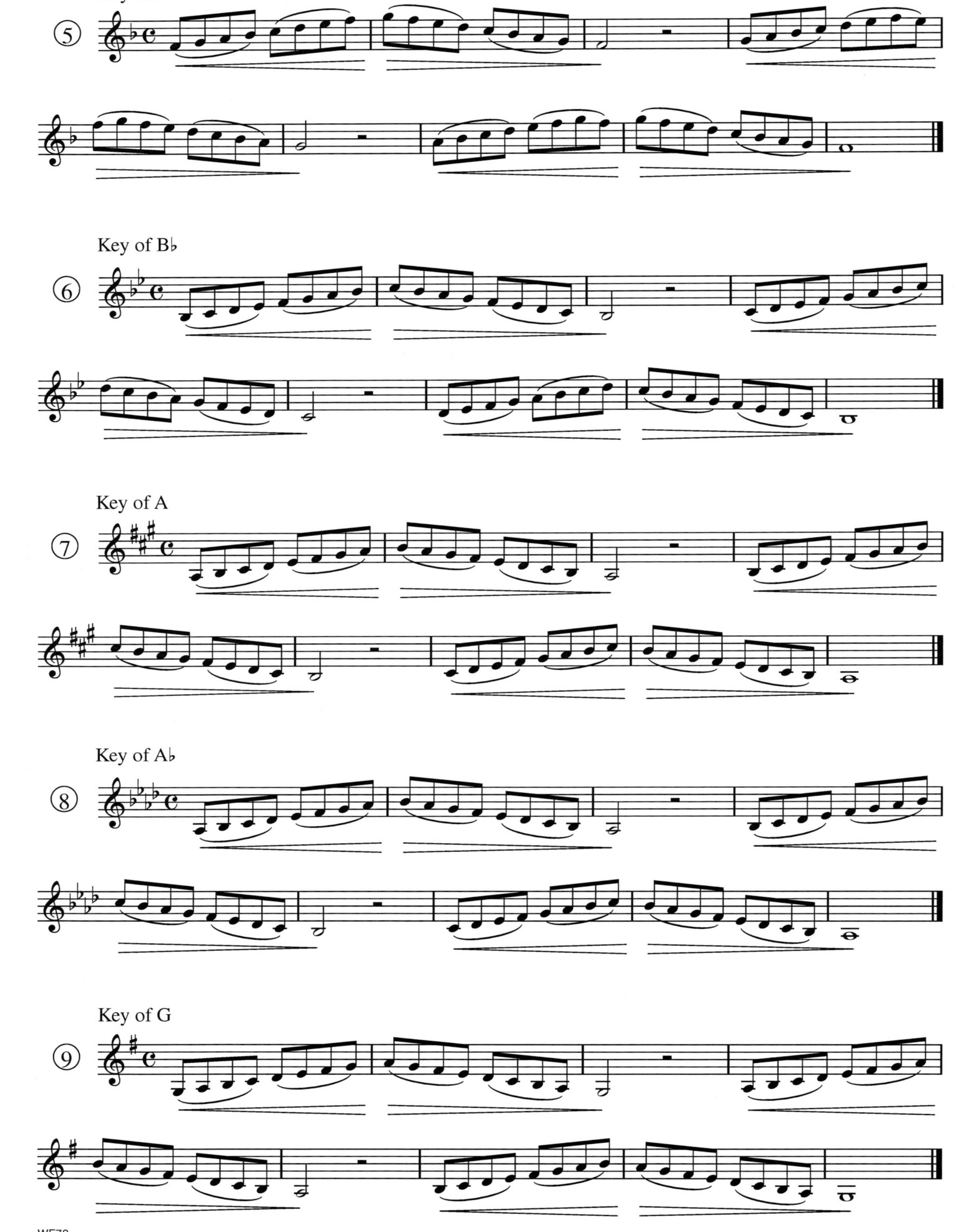
Key of F
5
Key of B♭
6
Key of A
7
Key of A♭
8
Key of G
9

Minor Scale Studies

correlates to page 83 in *Complete Conservatory Method*

1. For every major scale, there is a minor scale with the same key signature. It starts a minor third below the starting note for the major scale.
2. Minor scales come in three forms: a) pure, or natural minor; b) harmonic minor; or c) melodic minor.

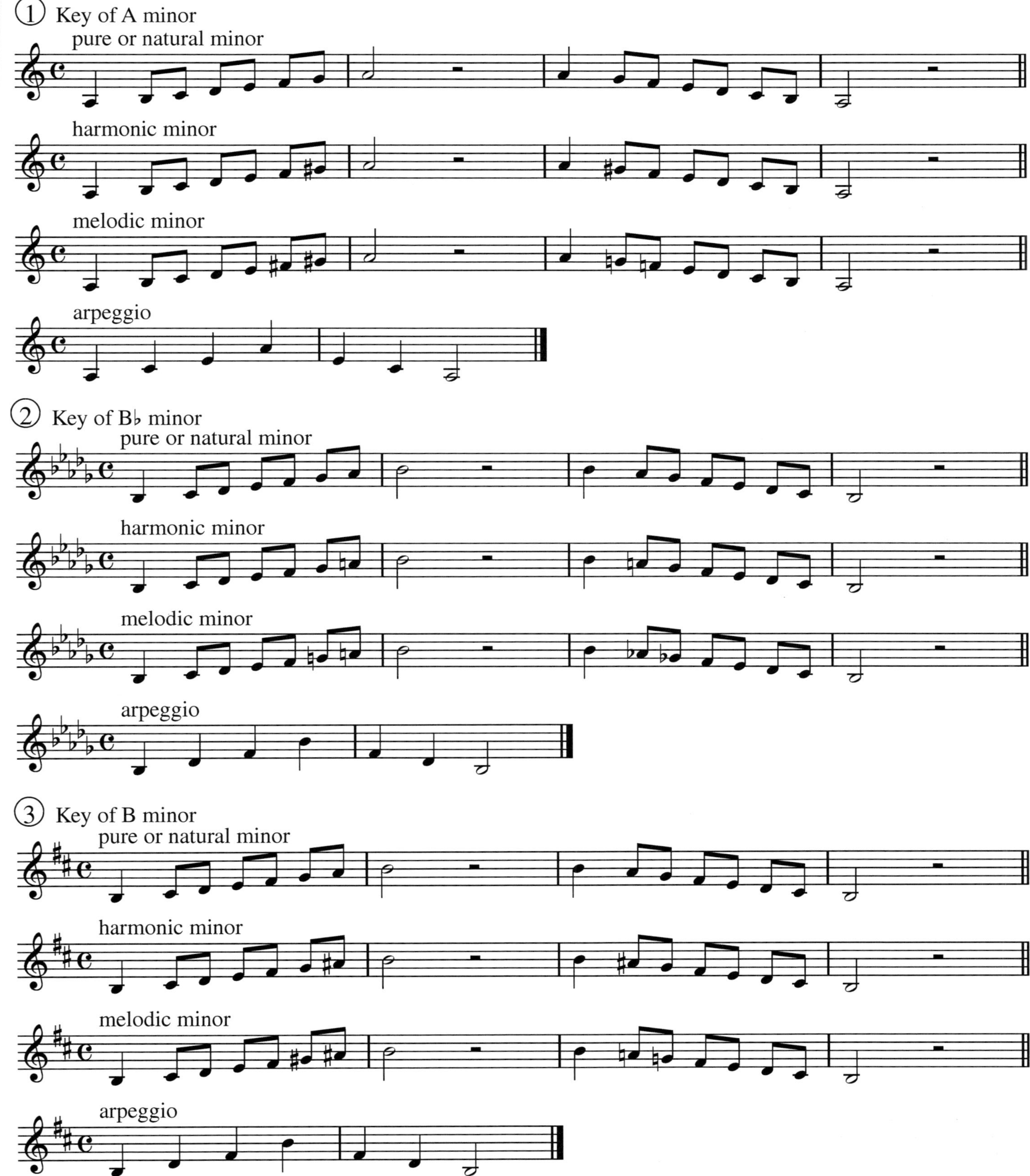

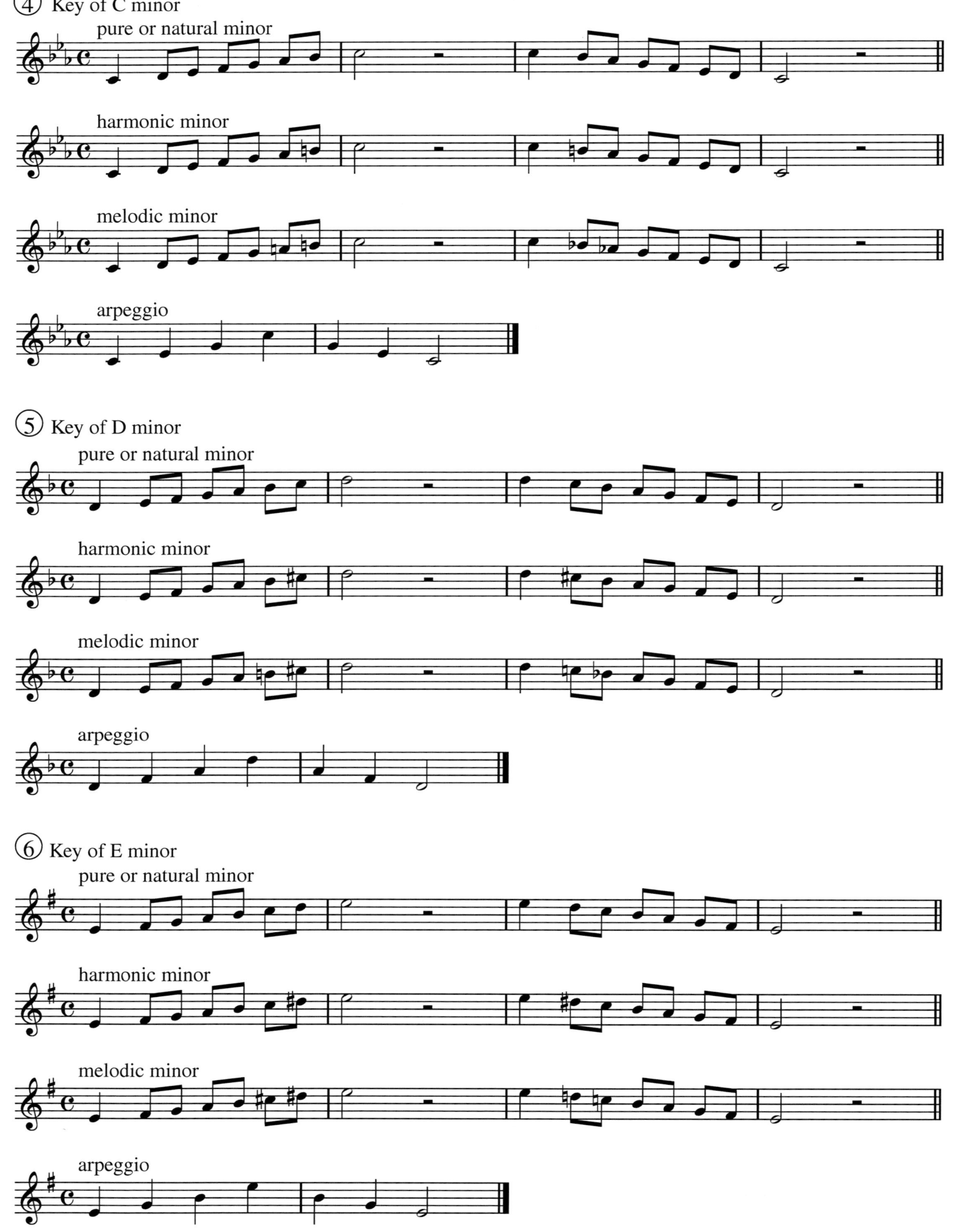
④ Key of C minor
pure or natural minor
harmonic minor
melodic minor
arpeggio
⑤ Key of D minor
pure or natural minor
harmonic minor
melodic minor
arpeggio
⑥ Key of E minor
pure or natural minor
harmonic minor
melodic minor
arpeggio

⑦ Key of F minor

pure or natural minor

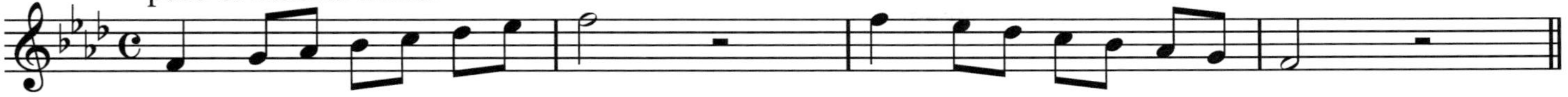

harmonic minor

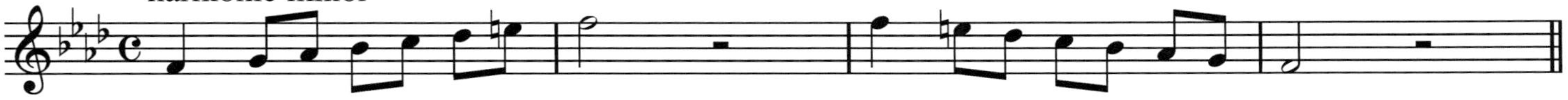

melodic minor

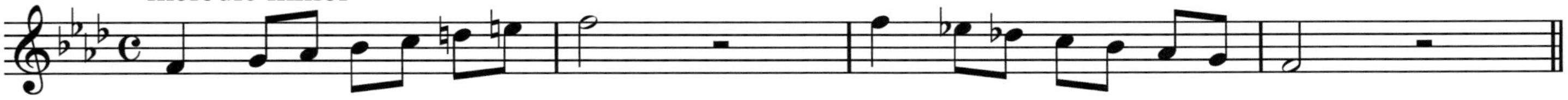

arpeggio

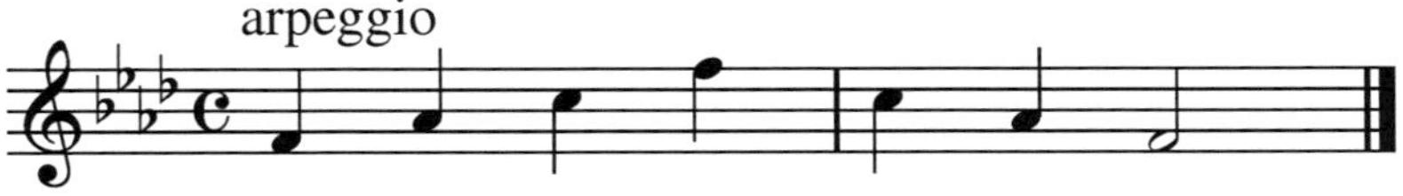

⑧ Key of F♯ minor

pure or natural minor

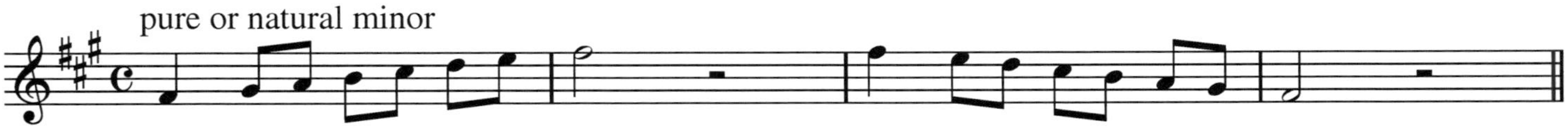

harmonic minor

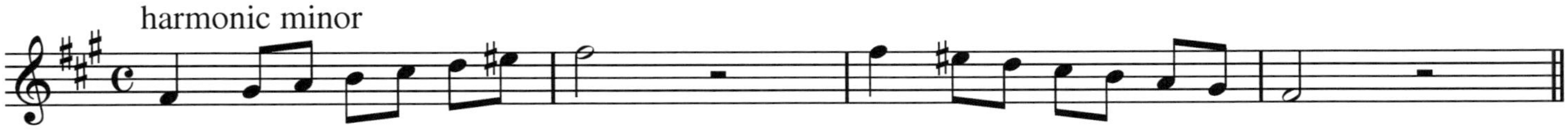

melodic minor

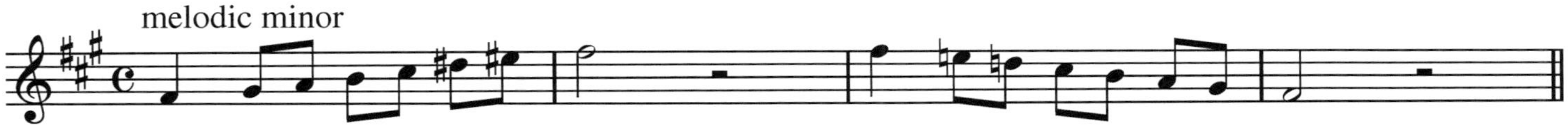

arpeggio

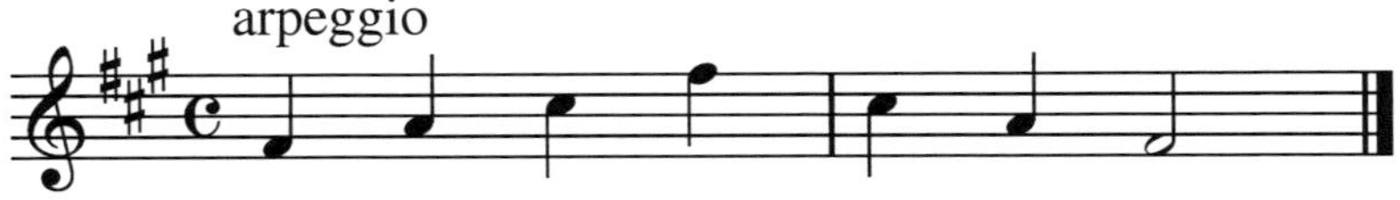

⑨ Key of G minor

pure or natural minor

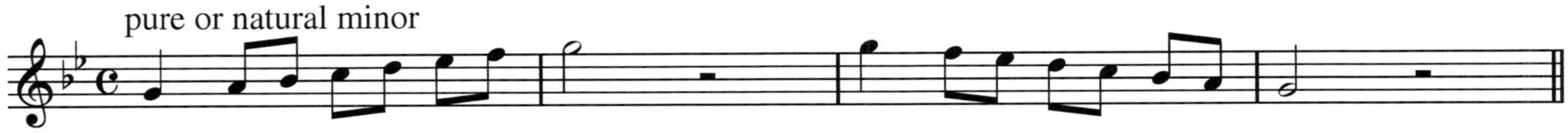

harmonic minor

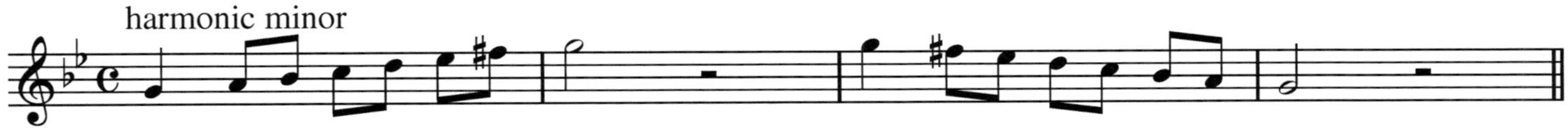

melodic minor

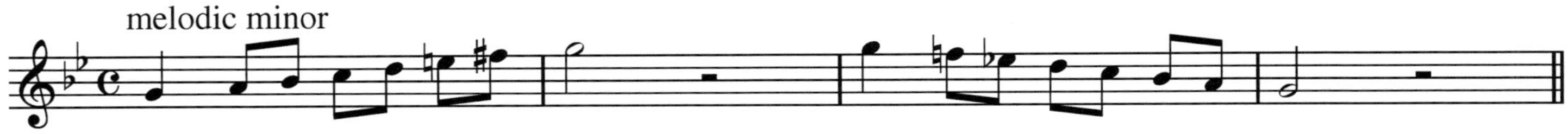

arpeggio

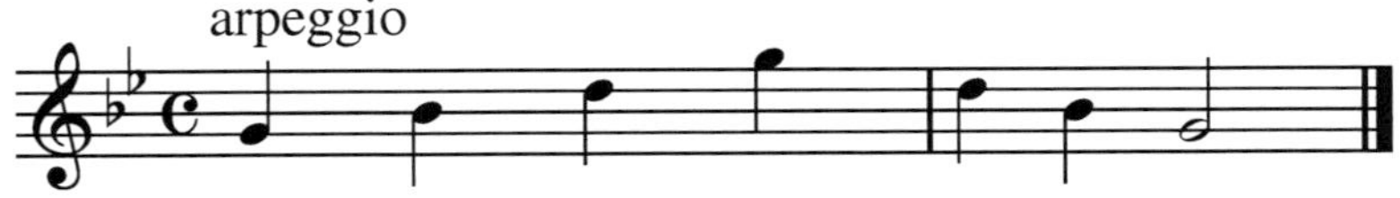

Chromatic Scale Studies

correlates to page 85 in *Complete Conservatory Method*

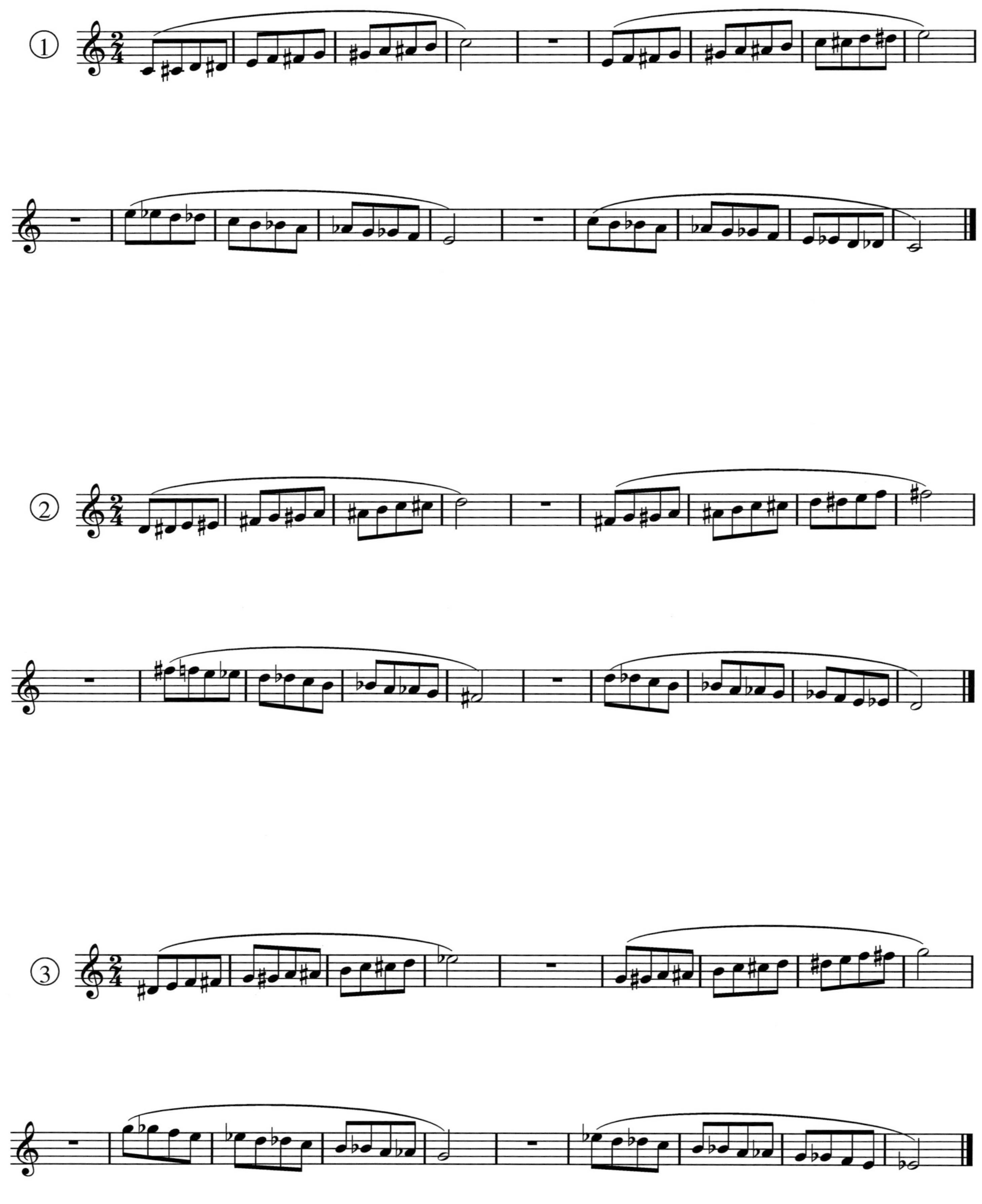

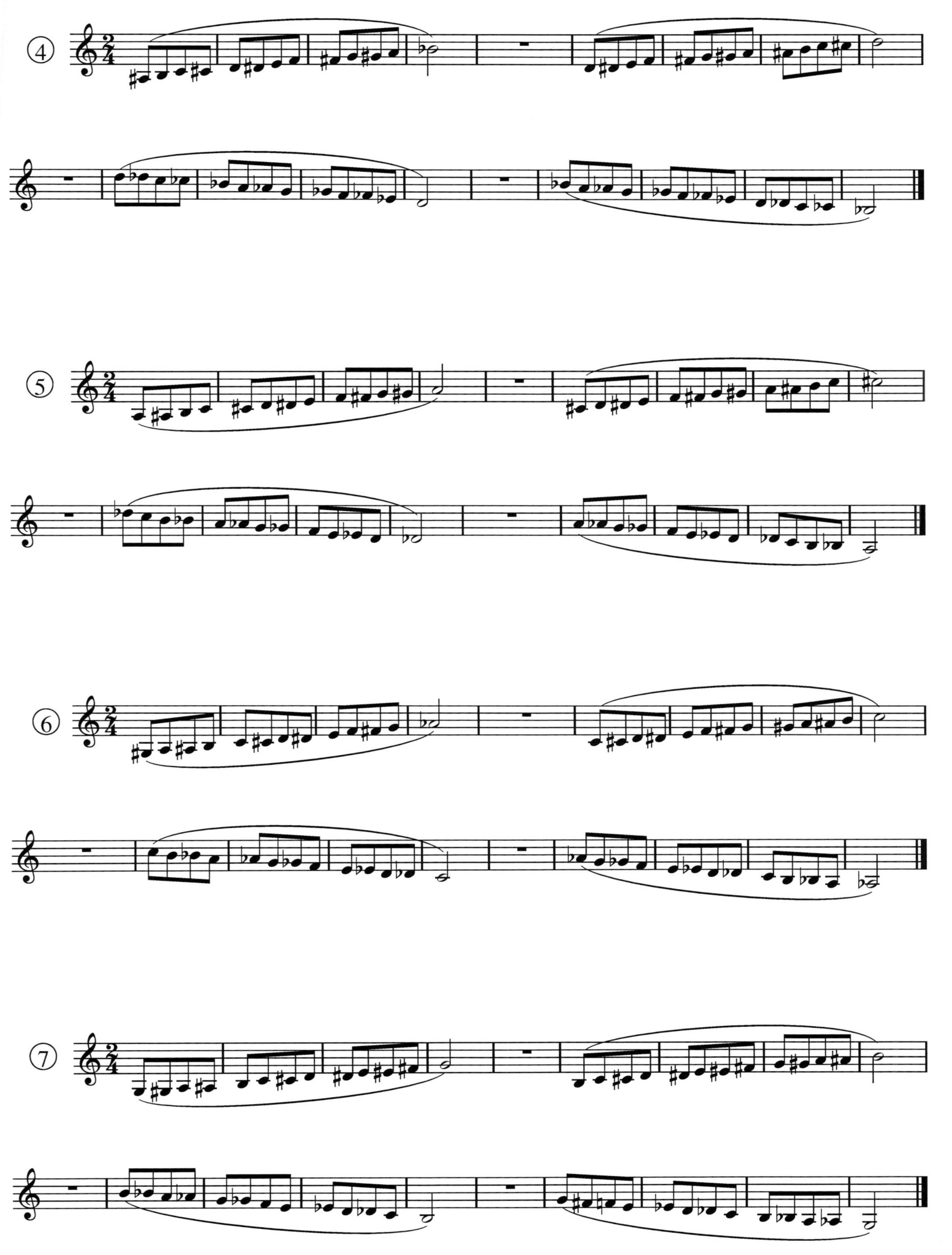
4
5
6
7

Preparatory Exercises on the Turn

correlates to page 100 in *Complete Conservatory Method*

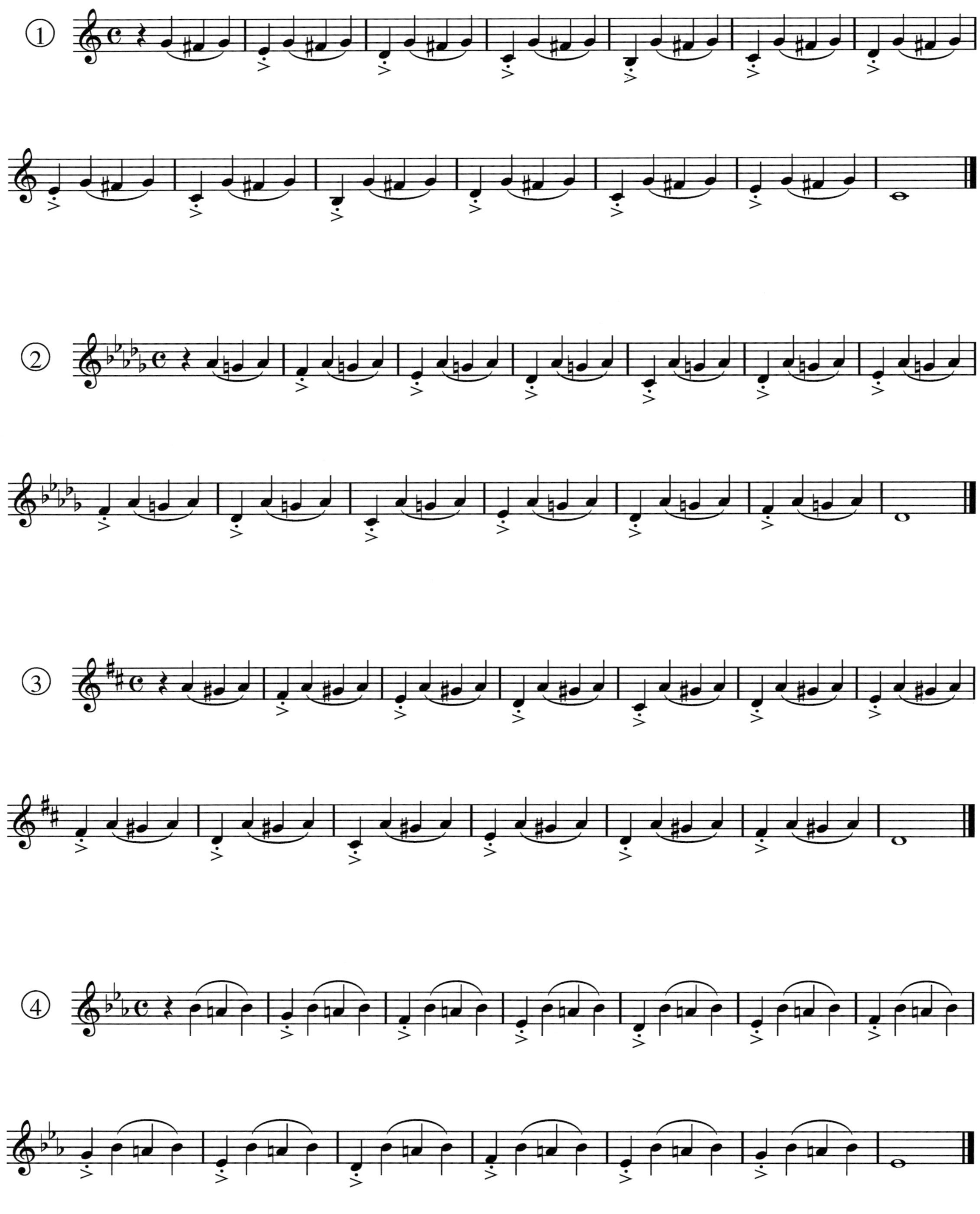

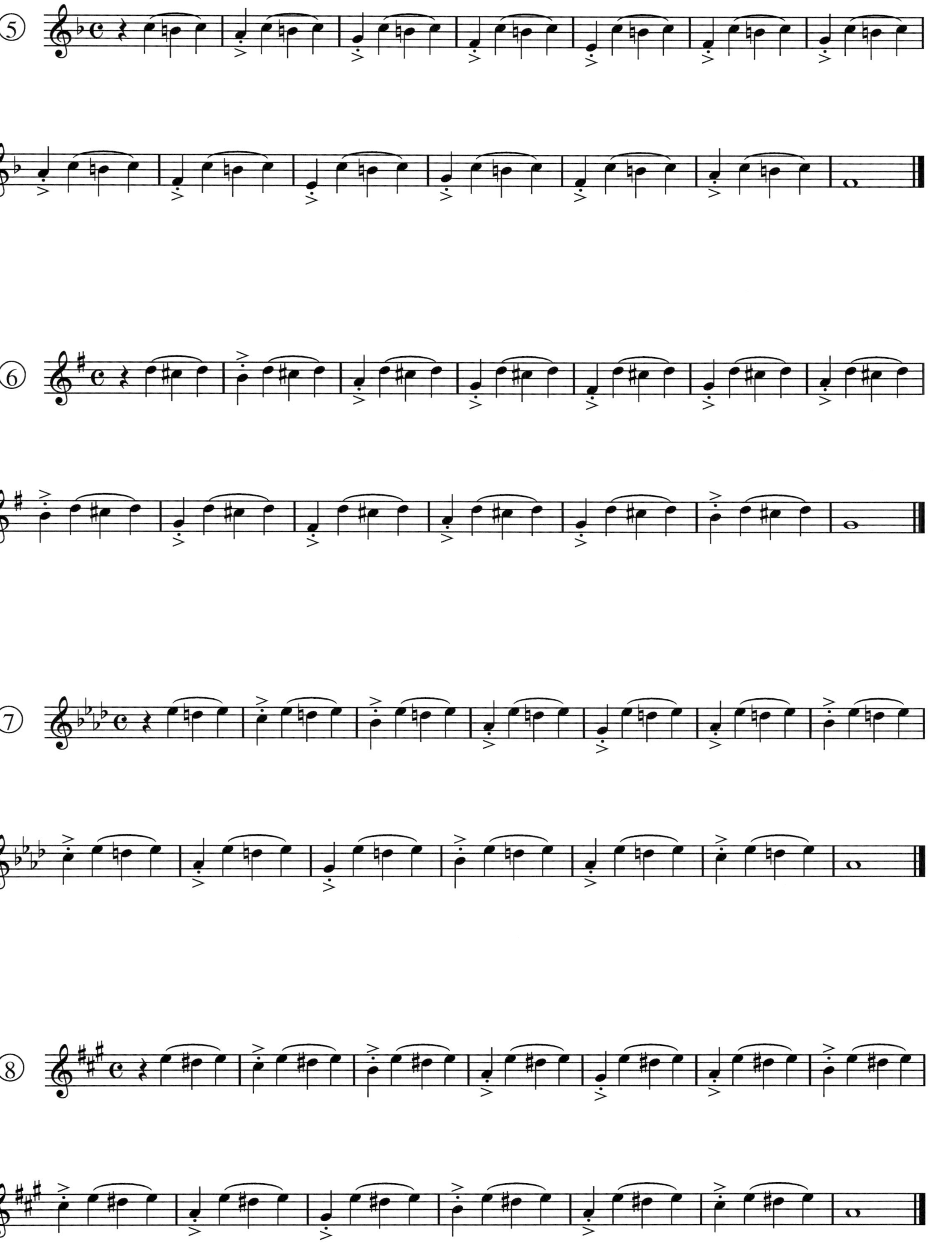
5
6
7
8

Intervals

correlates to page 144 in *Complete Conservatory Method*

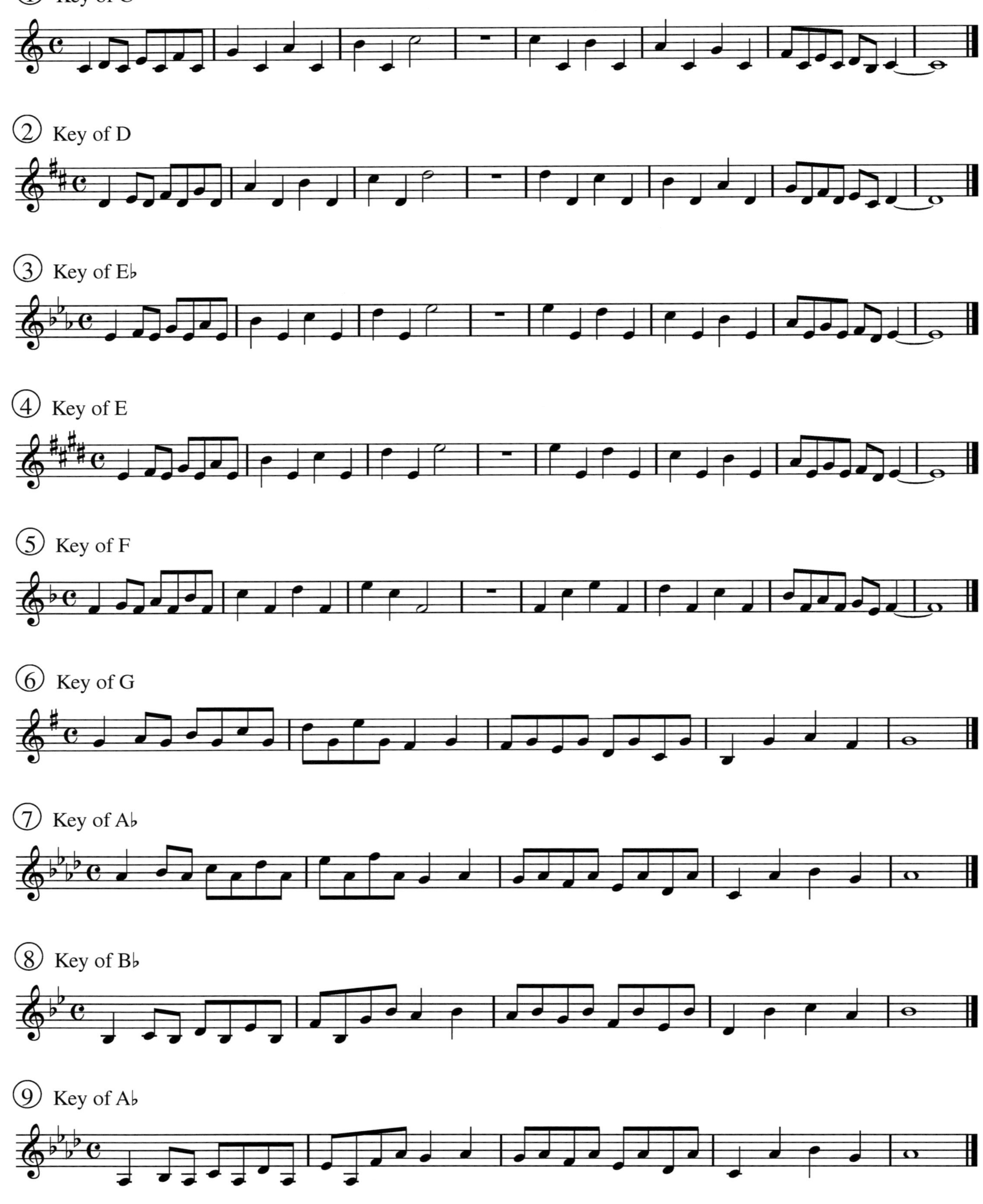

More Intervals

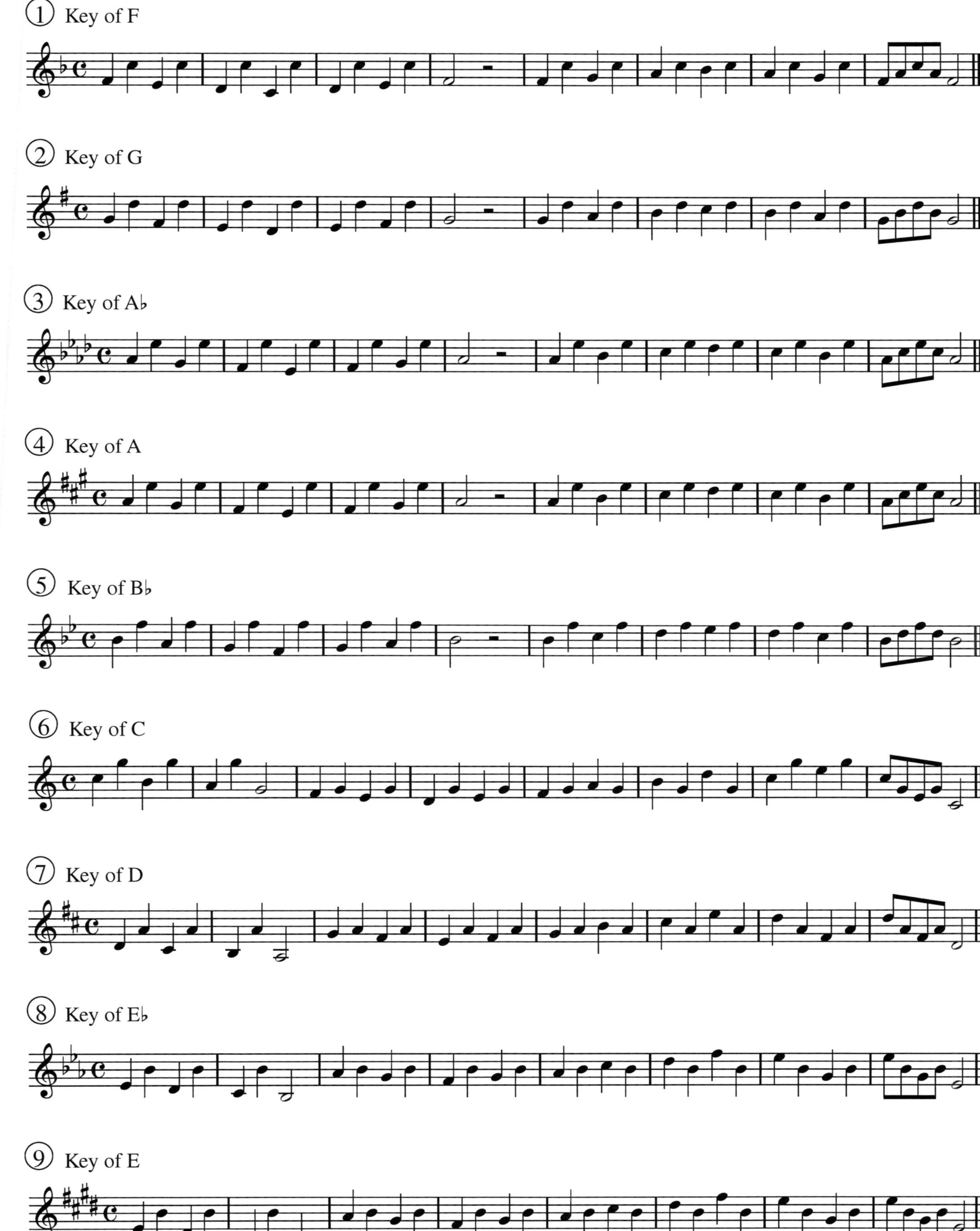

Major and Minor Arpeggios

correlates to page 170 in *Complete Conservatory Method*

① Key of C

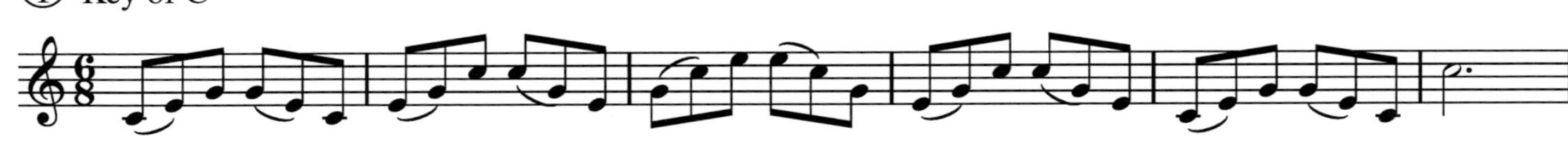

② Key of C minor

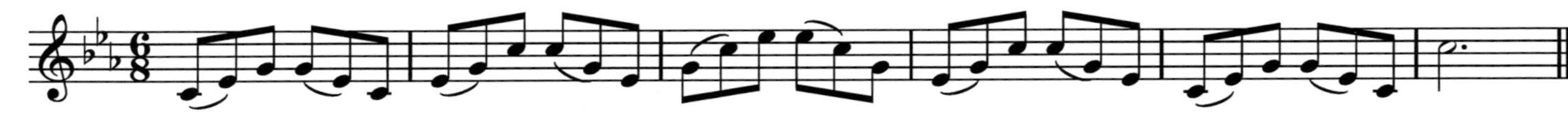

③ Key of D

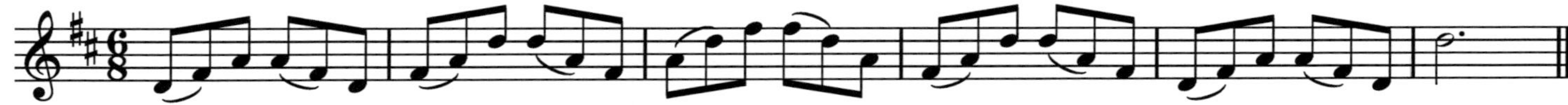

④ Key of D minor

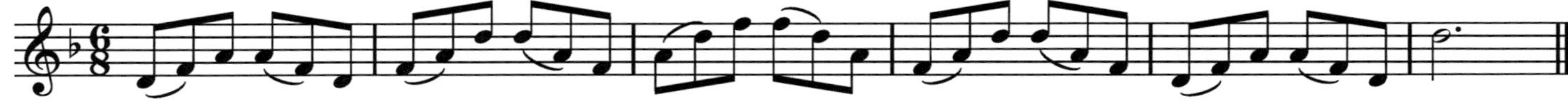

⑤ Key of E♭

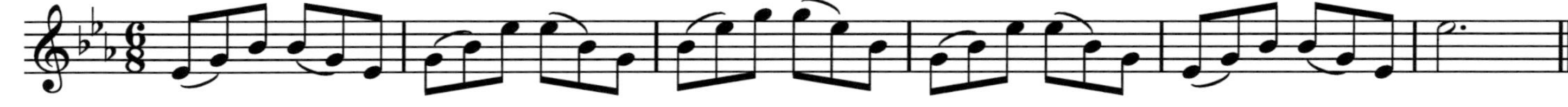

⑥ Key of E minor

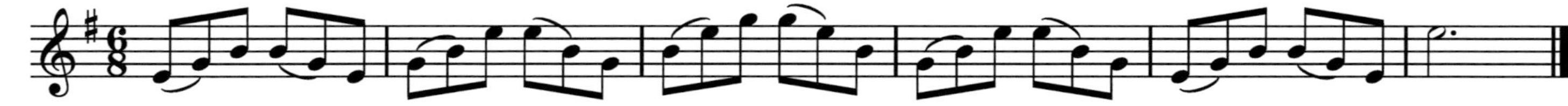

⑦ Key of F

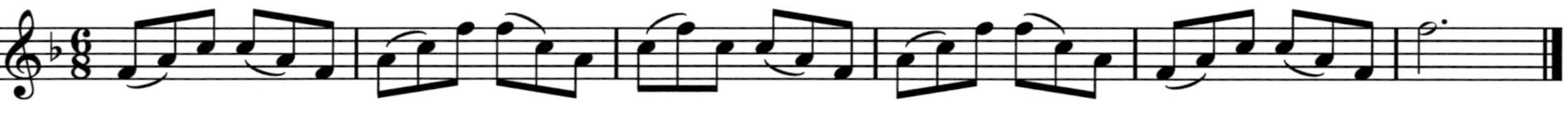

⑧ Key of F minor

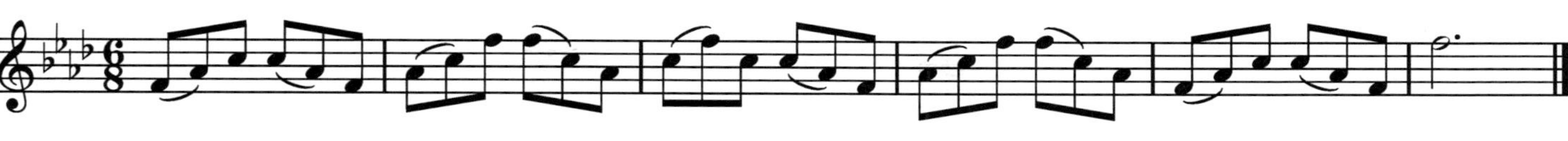

⑨ Key of G

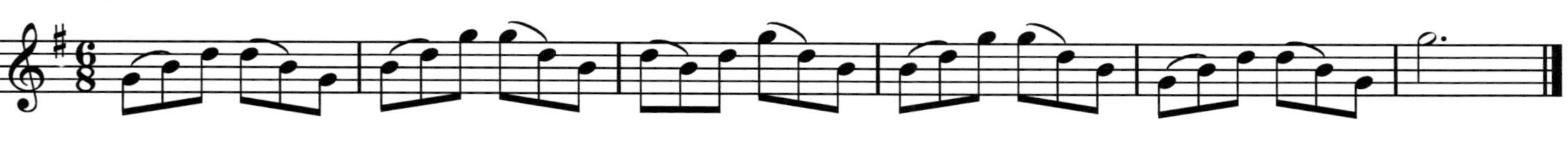

⑩ Key of G minor

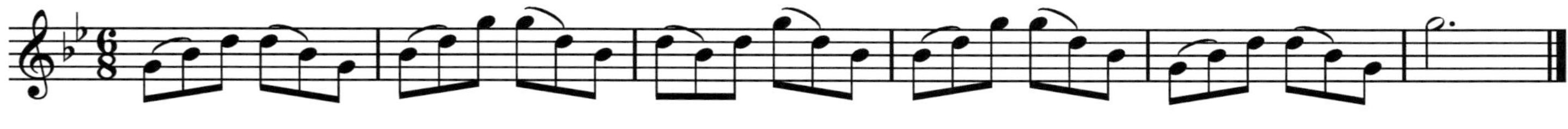

⑪ Key of B♭

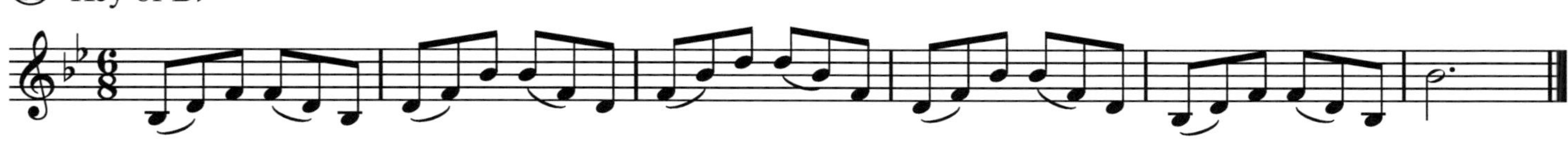

⑫ Key of A

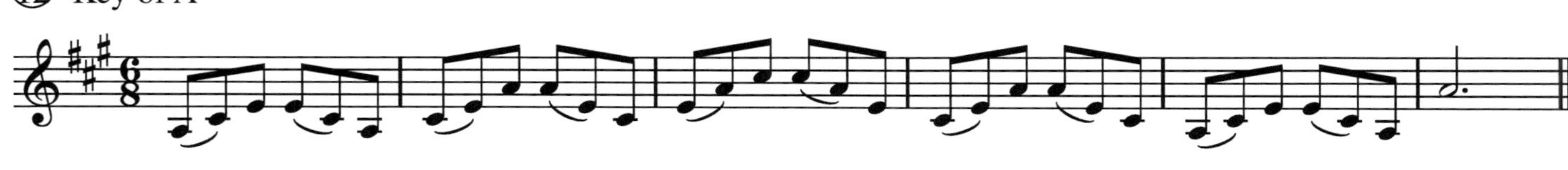

⑬ Key of A minor

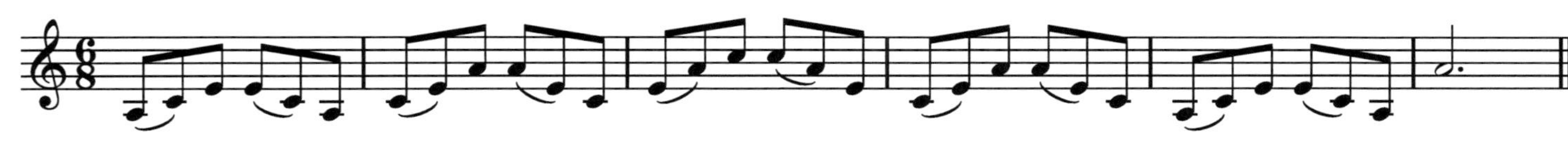

⑭ Key of A♭

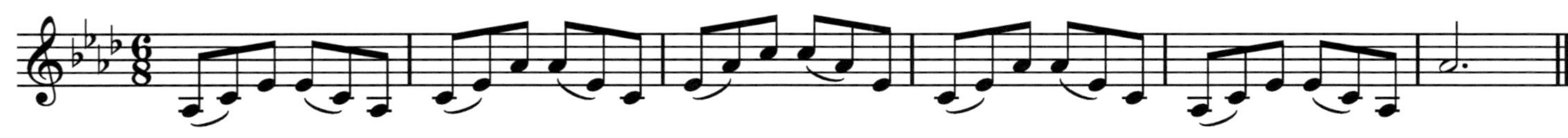

⑮ Key of A♭ minor

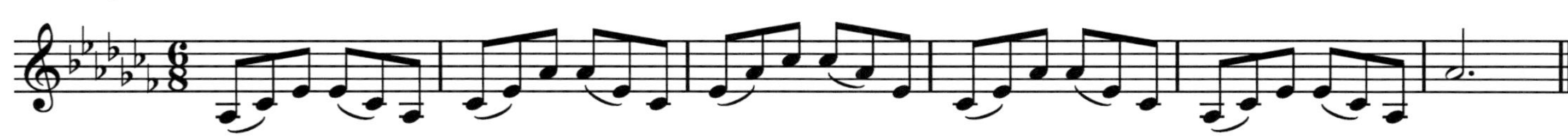

Triple Tonguing

correlates to page 189 in *Complete Conservatory Method*

Three easy steps to triple tonguing:
1. Say the syllables; then *sing* it.
2. *Buzz* it: a) without mouthpiece; b) with mouthpiece.
3. *Play* it.
NOTE: Apply all three steps to each exercise.

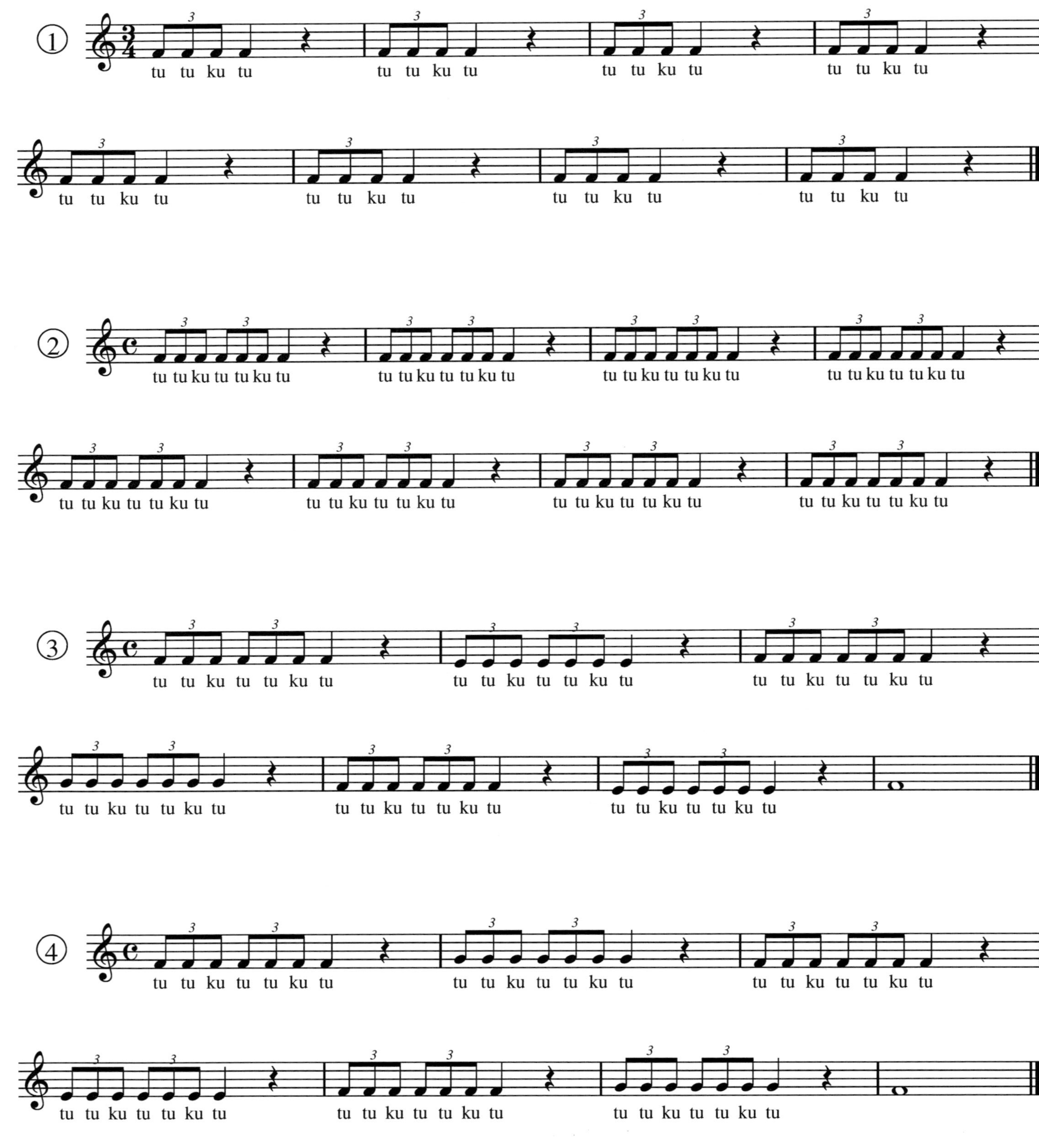

⑤

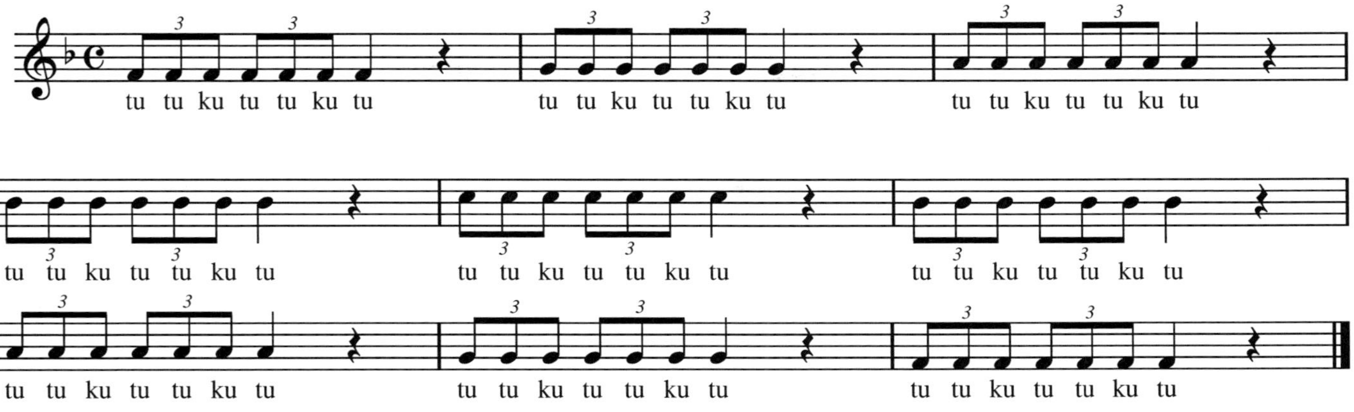

tu tu ku tu tu ku tu | tu tu ku tu tu ku tu | tu tu ku tu tu ku tu

tu tu ku tu tu ku tu | tu tu ku tu tu ku tu | tu tu ku tu tu ku tu

tu tu ku tu tu ku tu | tu tu ku tu tu ku tu | tu tu ku tu tu ku tu

⑥

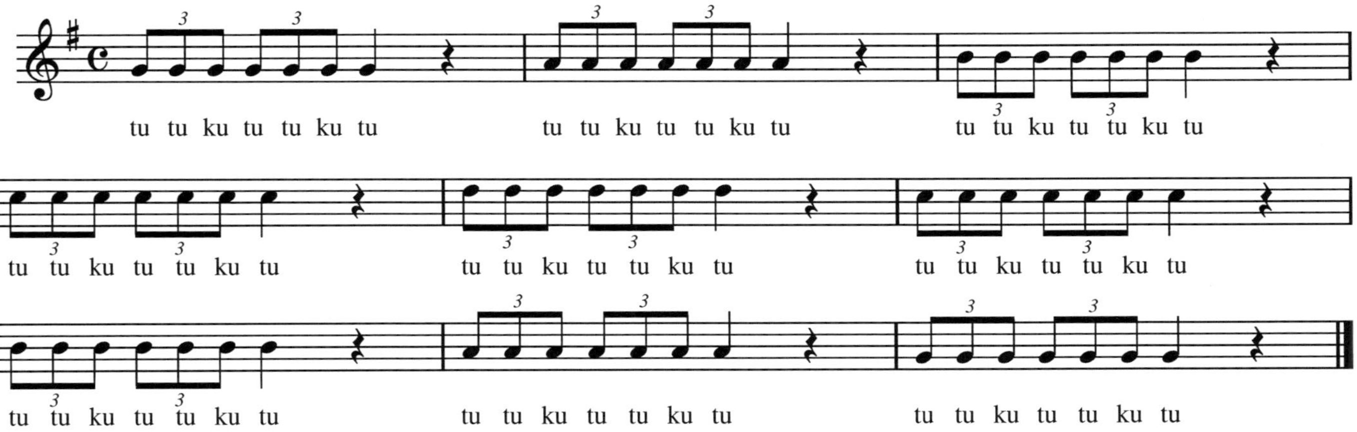

tu tu ku tu tu ku tu | tu tu ku tu tu ku tu | tu tu ku tu tu ku tu

tu tu ku tu tu ku tu | tu tu ku tu tu ku tu | tu tu ku tu tu ku tu

tu tu ku tu tu ku tu | tu tu ku tu tu ku tu | tu tu ku tu tu ku tu

⑦

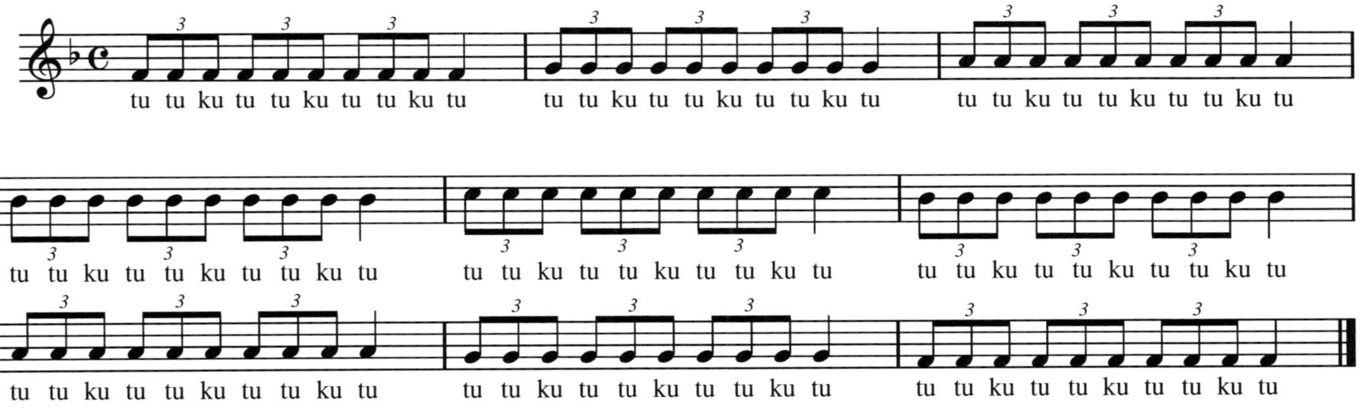

tu tu ku tu tu ku tu tu ku tu | tu tu ku tu tu ku tu tu ku tu | tu tu ku tu tu ku tu tu ku tu

tu tu ku tu tu ku tu tu ku tu | tu tu ku tu tu ku tu tu ku tu | tu tu ku tu tu ku tu tu ku tu

tu tu ku tu tu ku tu tu ku tu | tu tu ku tu tu ku tu tu ku tu | tu tu ku tu tu ku tu tu ku tu

⑧

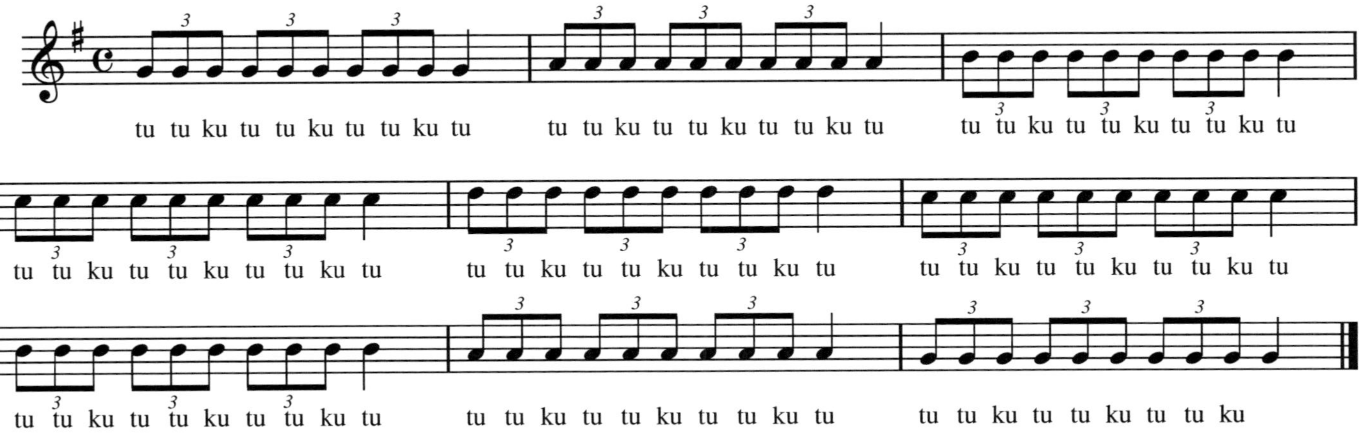

tu tu ku tu tu ku tu tu ku tu | tu tu ku tu tu ku tu tu ku tu | tu tu ku tu tu ku tu tu ku tu

tu tu ku tu tu ku tu tu ku tu | tu tu ku tu tu ku tu tu ku tu | tu tu ku tu tu ku tu tu ku tu

tu tu ku tu tu ku tu tu ku tu | tu tu ku tu tu ku tu tu ku tu | tu tu ku tu tu ku tu tu ku

Double Tonguing

correlates to page 214 in *Complete Conservatory Method*

Use the three steps given on page 36.

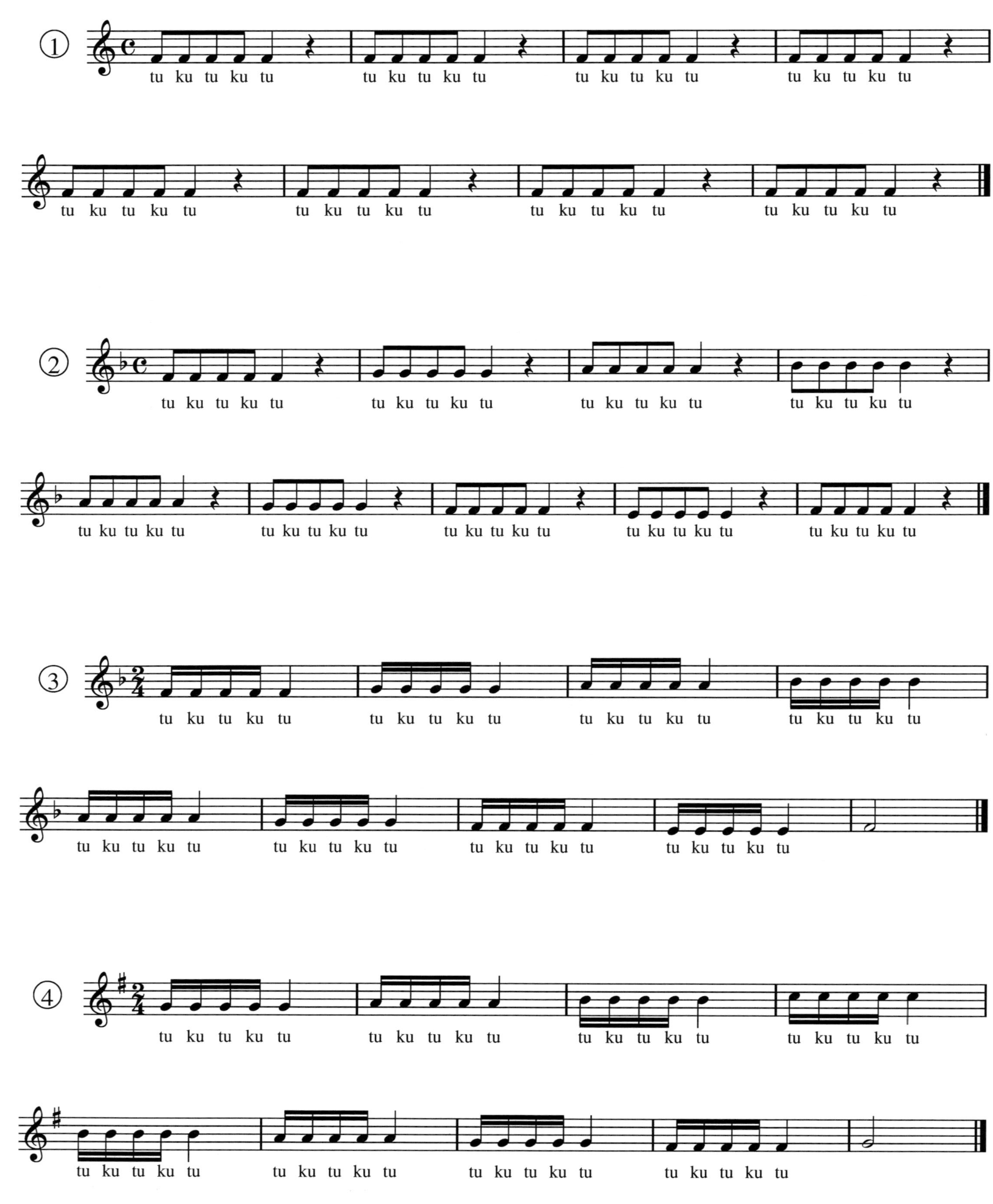

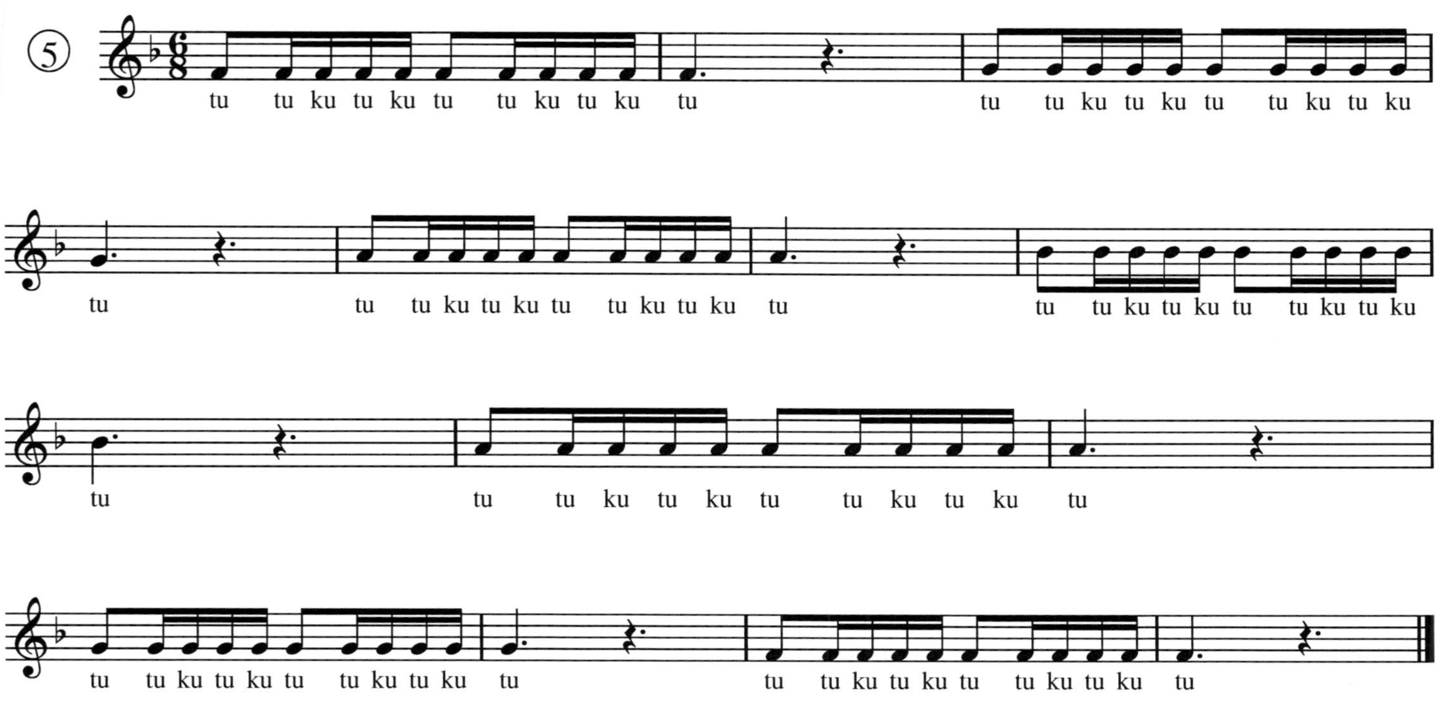

⑤

tu tu ku tu ku tu tu ku tu ku tu tu tu ku tu ku tu tu ku tu ku

tu tu tu ku tu ku tu tu ku tu ku tu tu tu ku tu ku tu tu ku tu ku

tu tu tu ku tu ku tu tu ku tu ku tu

tu tu ku tu ku tu tu ku tu ku tu tu tu ku tu ku tu tu ku tu ku tu

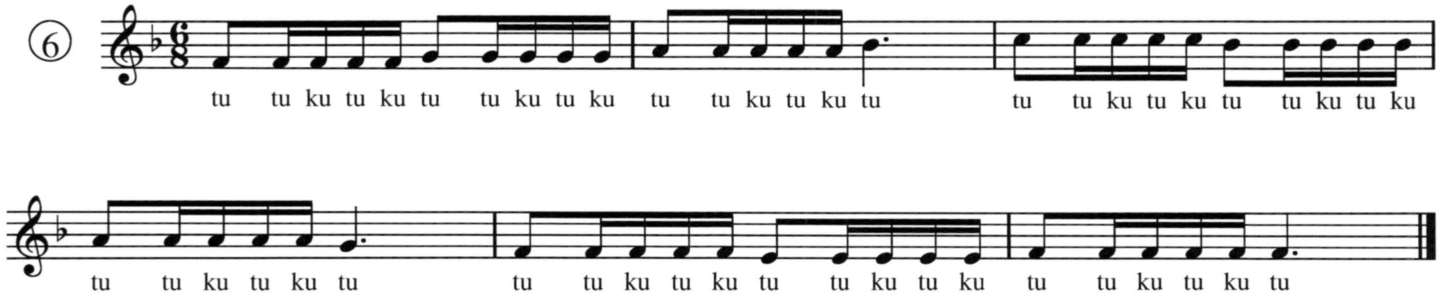

⑥

tu tu ku tu ku tu tu ku tu ku tu tu ku tu ku tu tu tu ku tu ku tu tu ku tu ku

tu tu ku tu ku tu tu tu ku tu ku tu tu ku tu ku tu tu ku tu ku tu

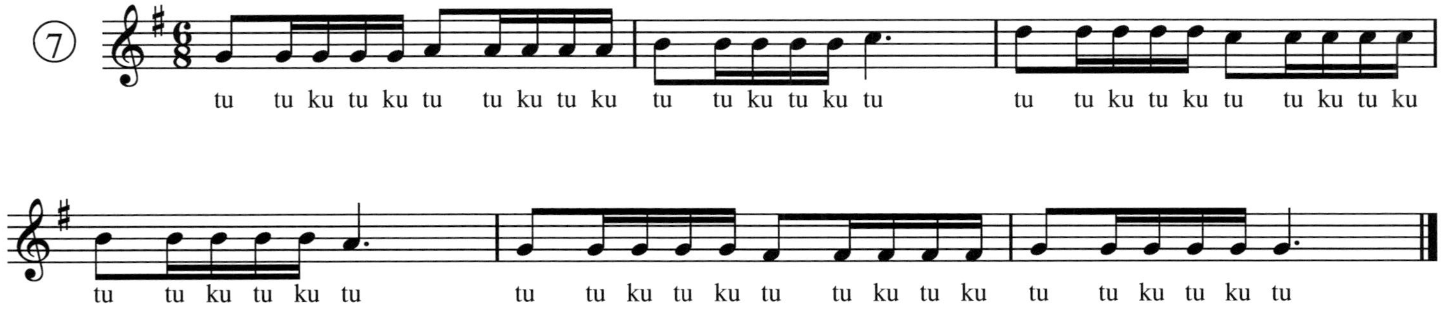

⑦

tu tu ku tu ku tu tu ku tu ku tu tu ku tu ku tu tu tu ku tu ku tu tu ku tu ku

tu tu ku tu ku tu tu tu ku tu ku tu tu ku tu ku tu tu ku tu ku tu

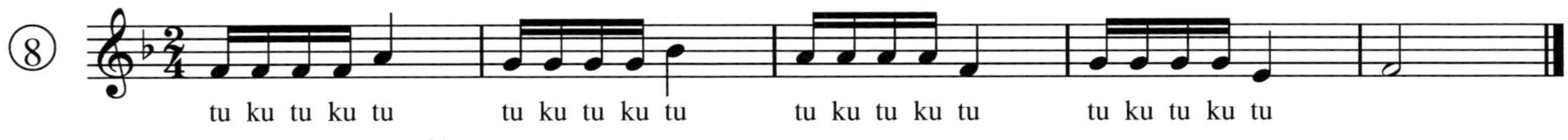

⑧

tu ku tu ku tu tu ku tu ku tu tu ku tu ku tu tu ku tu ku tu

The Art of Phrasing

correlates to page 232 in *Complete Conservatory Method*

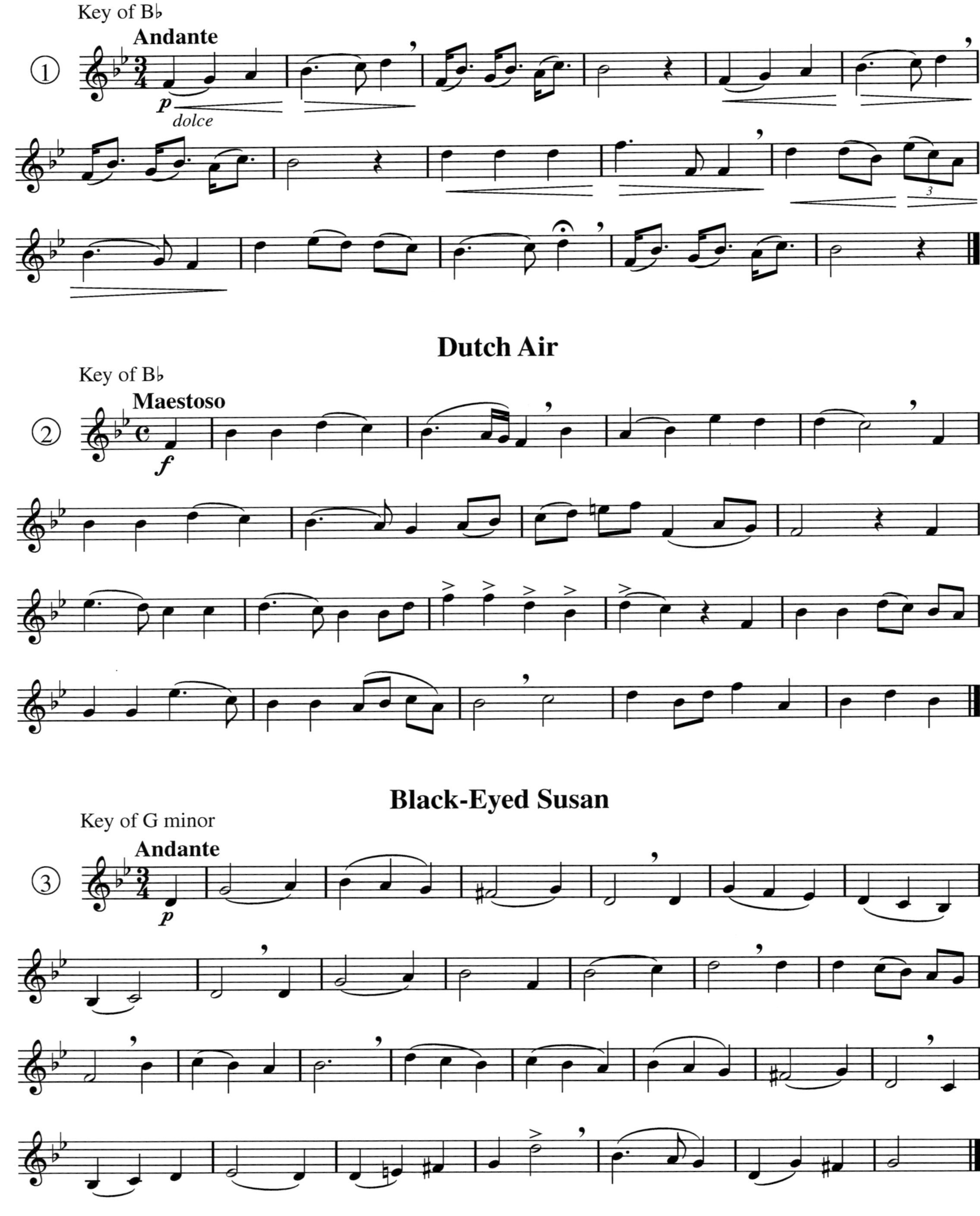

Le Desir

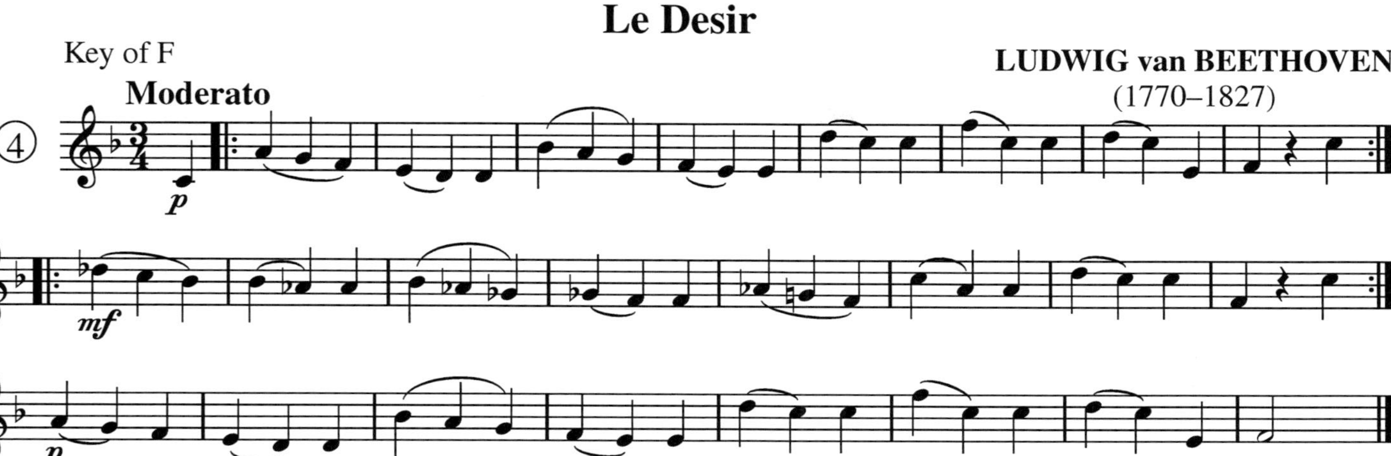

Romeo

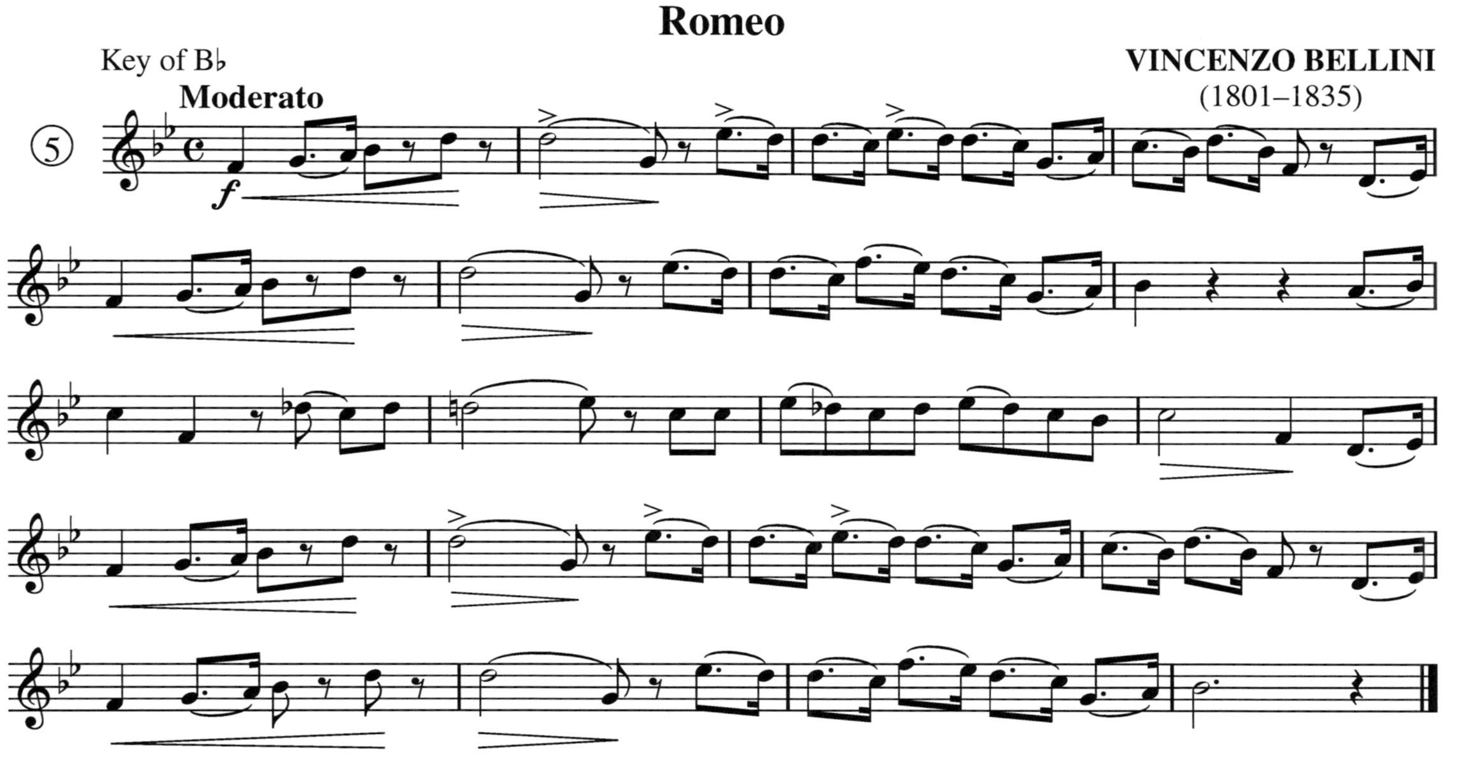

Serenade

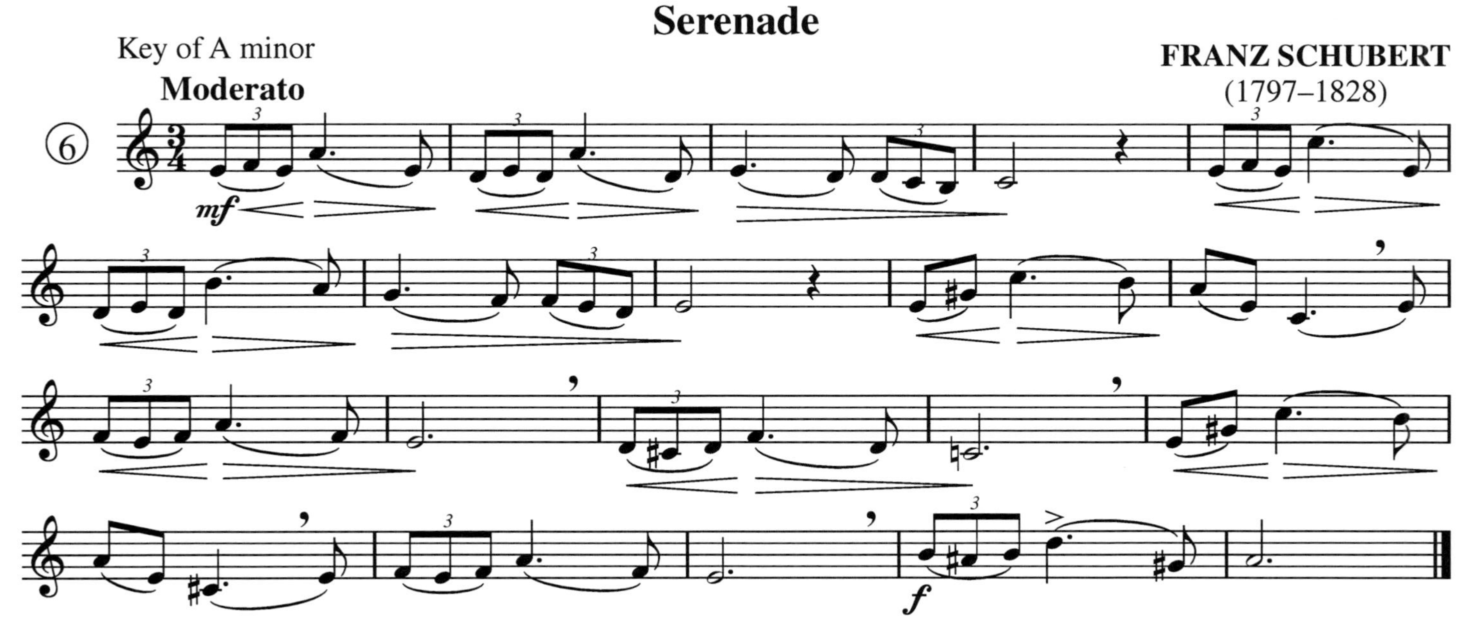

Duets for Two Cornets/Trumpets

correlates to page 306 in *Complete Conservatory Method*

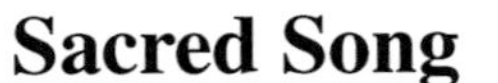

PORTNIANSKY

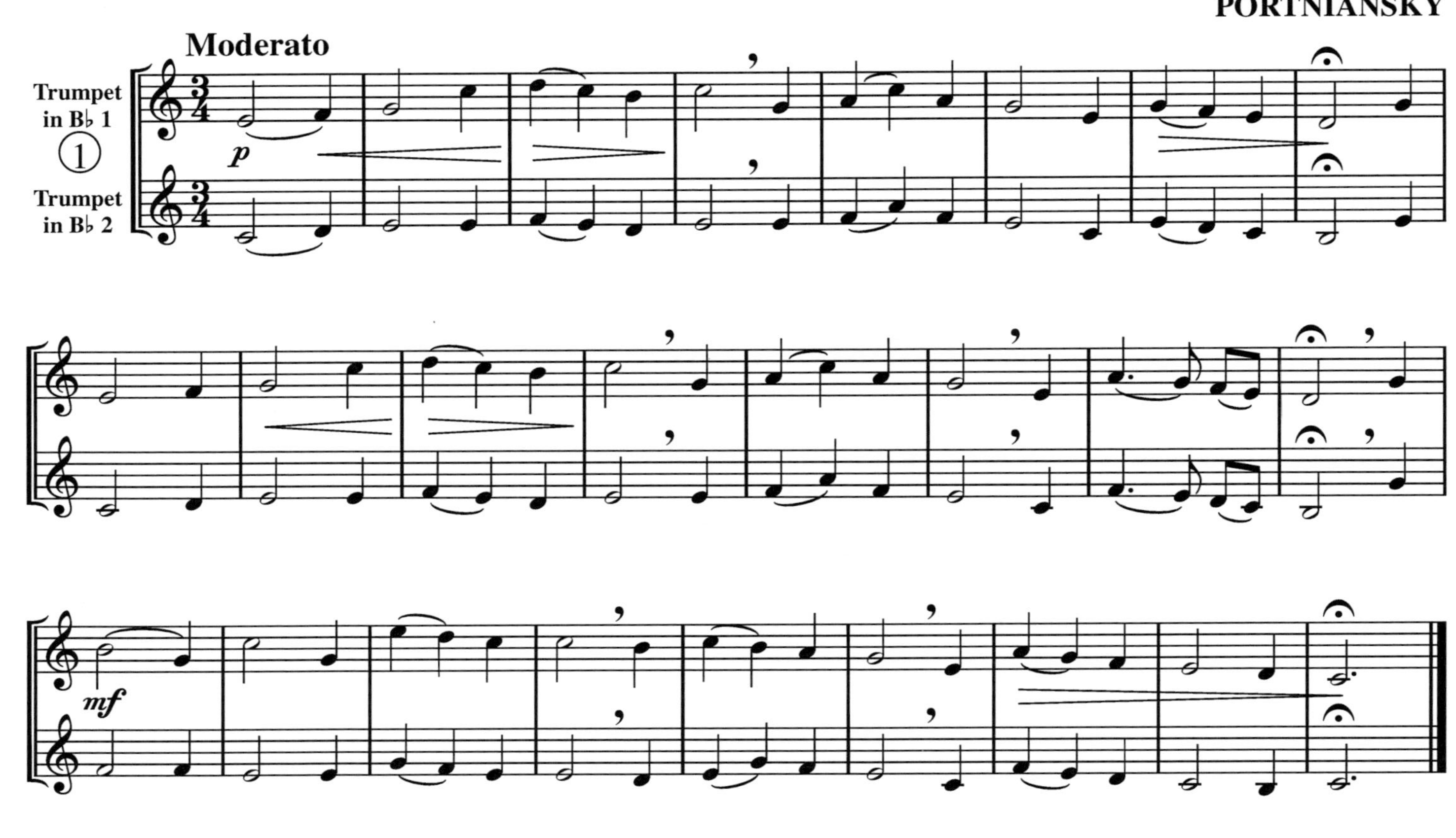

Melody

SALVERIO

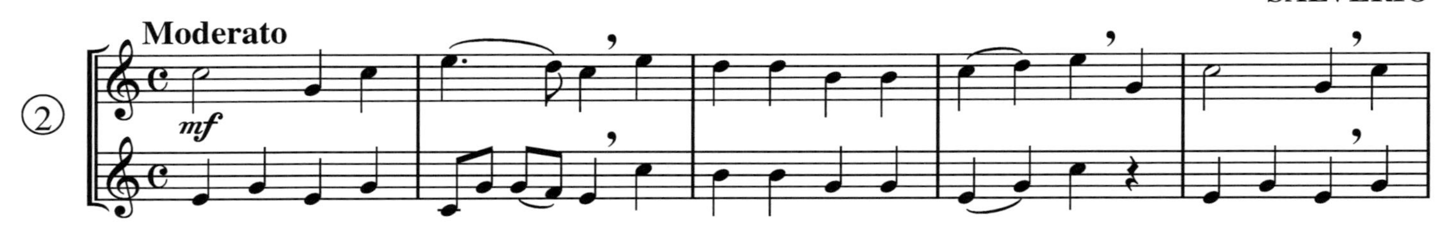

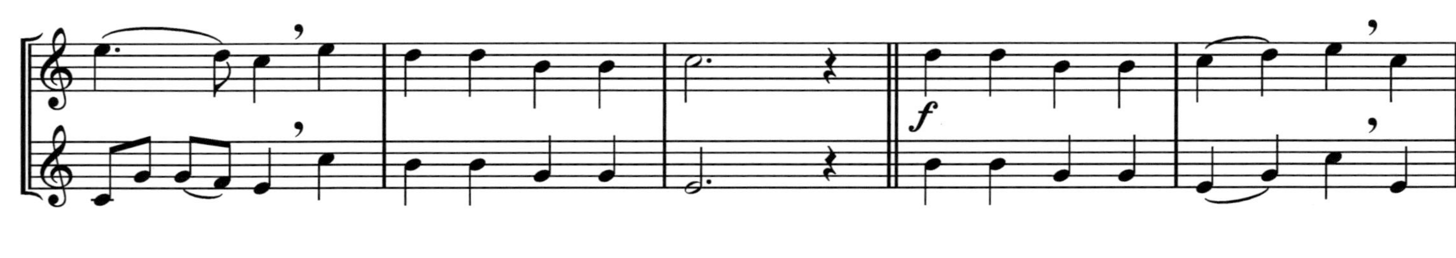

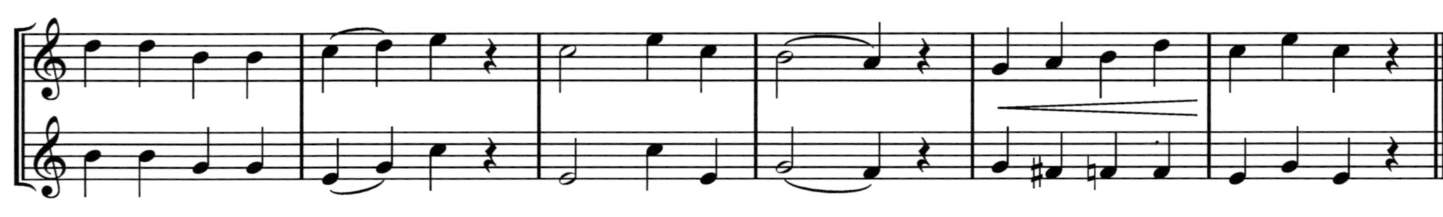

Air

WOLFGANG AMADEUS MOZART
(1756–1791)

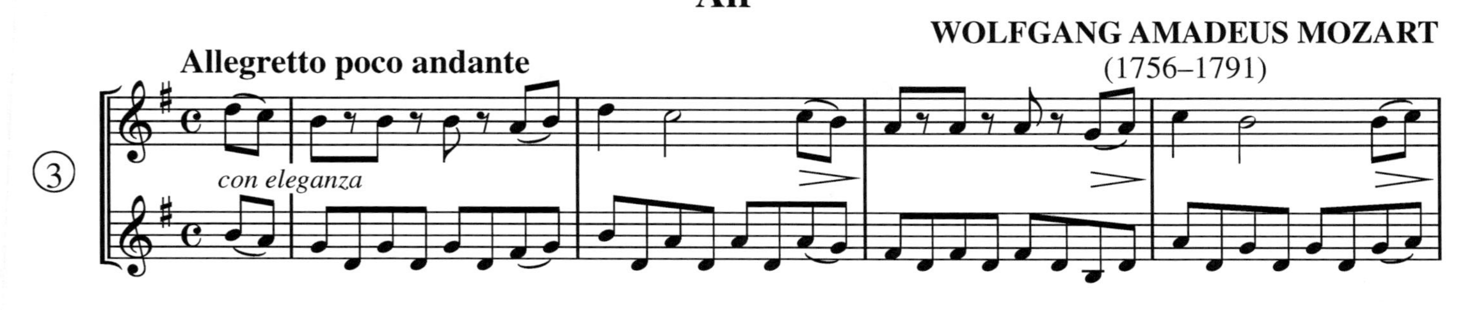

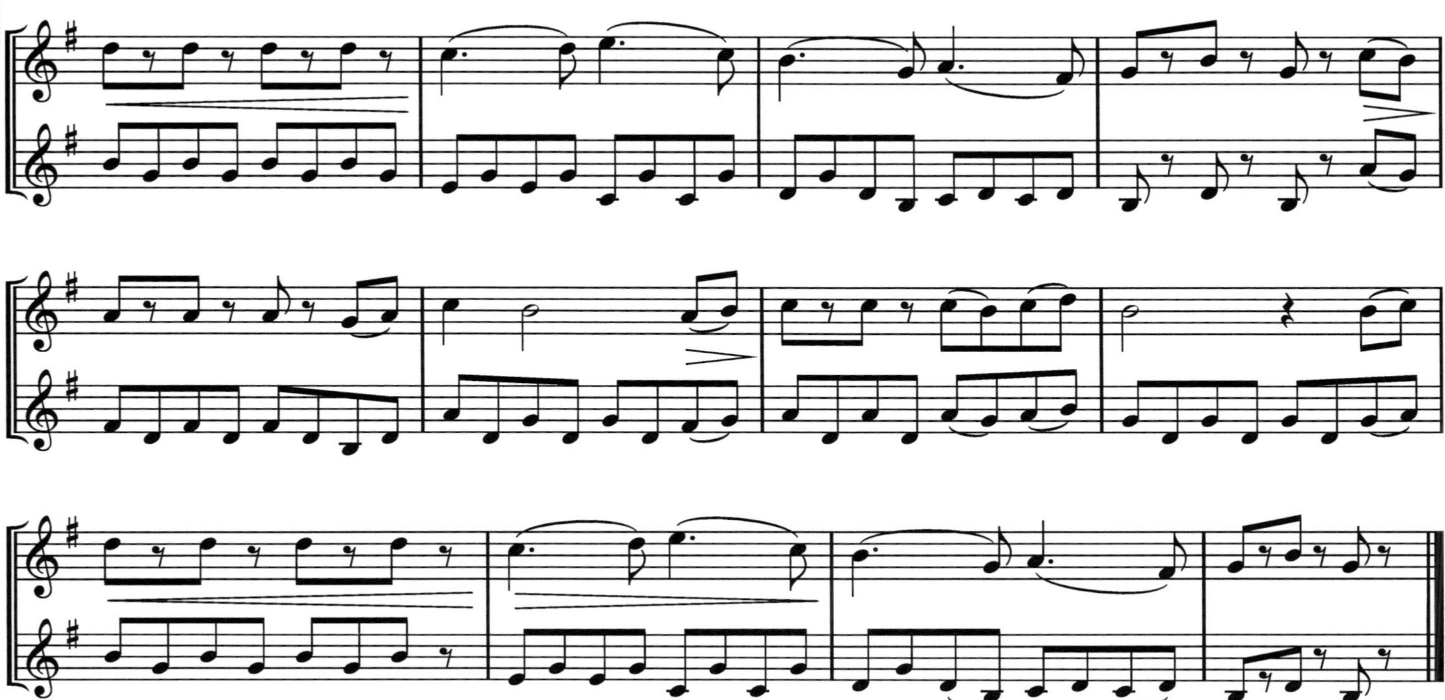

Arabian Song

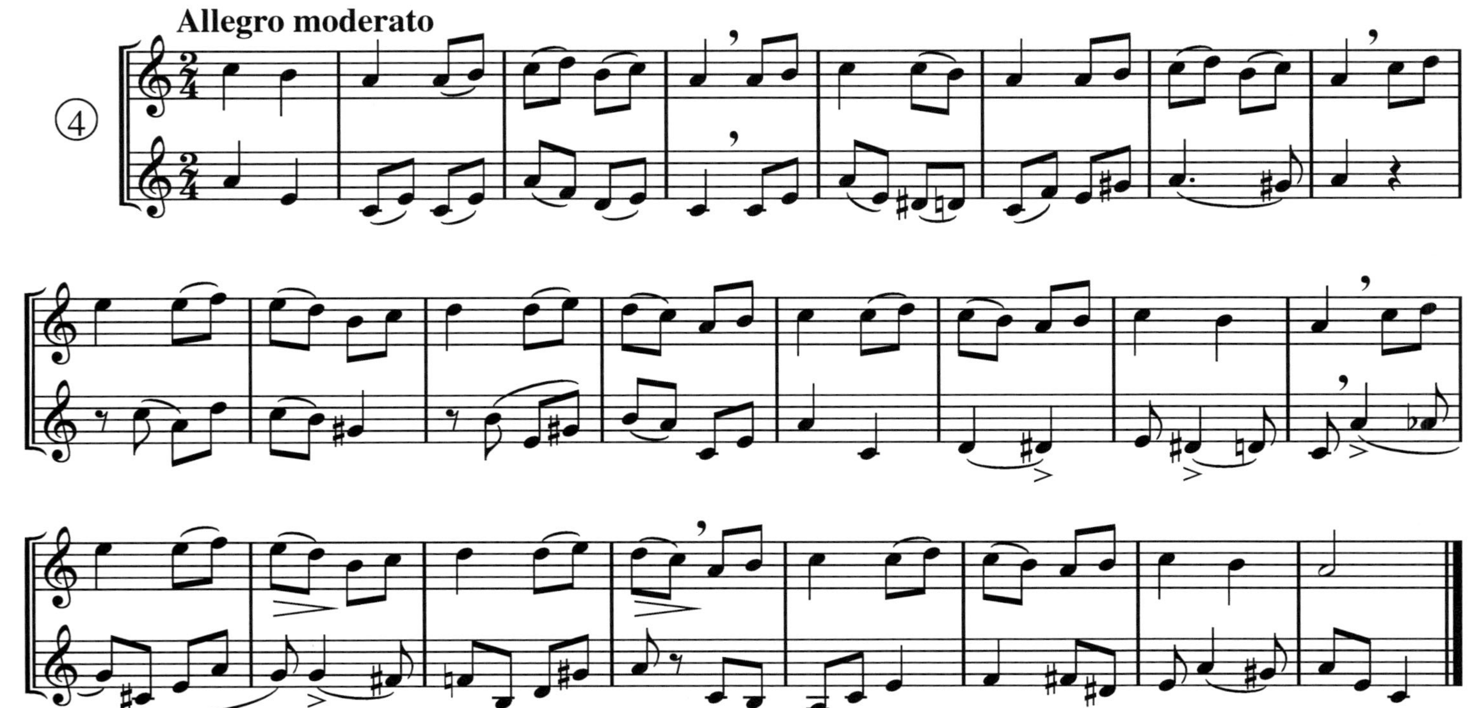

Serenade

GRETRY

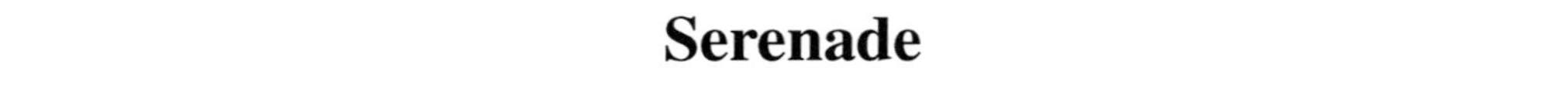

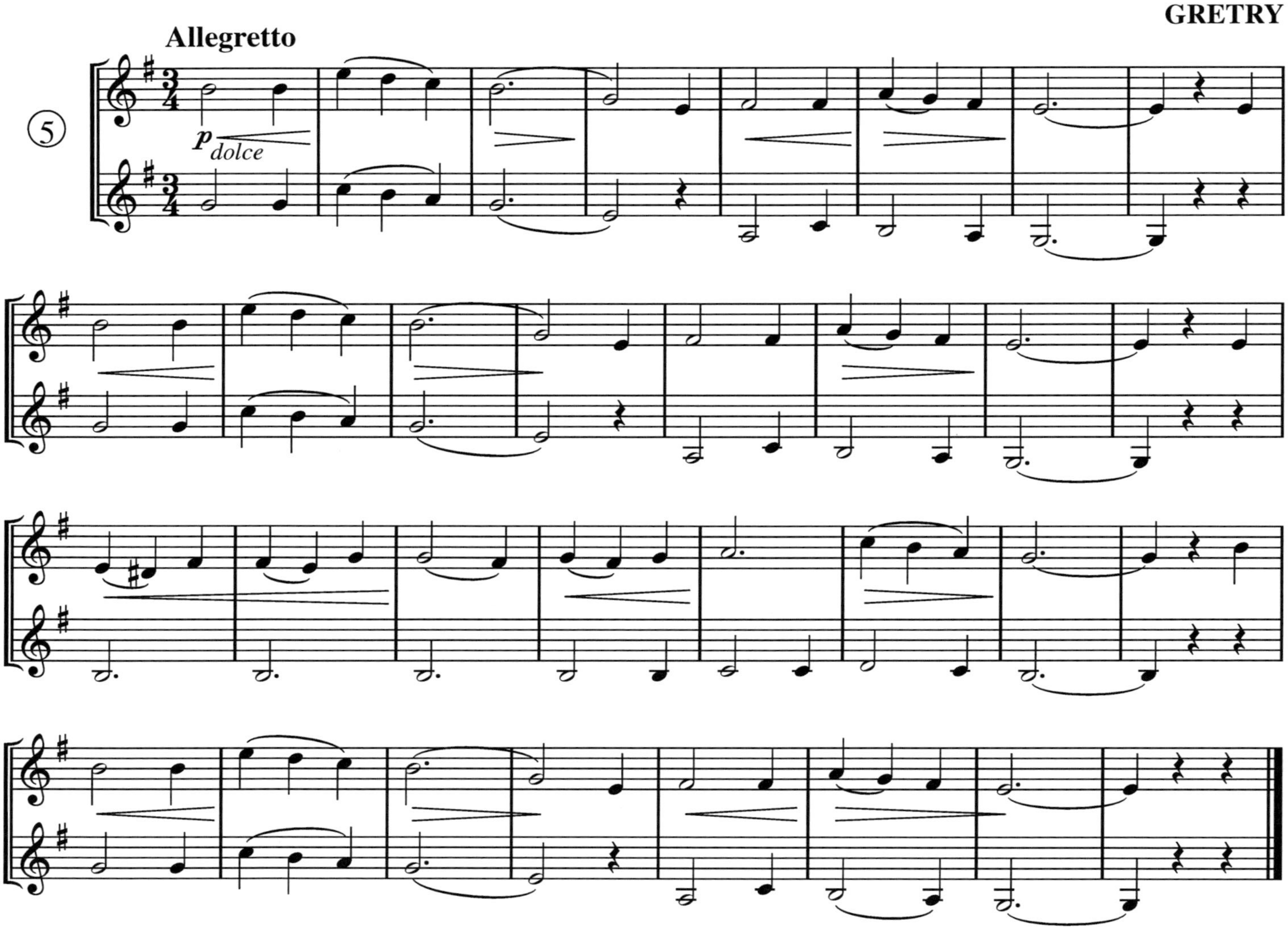

La Romanesca

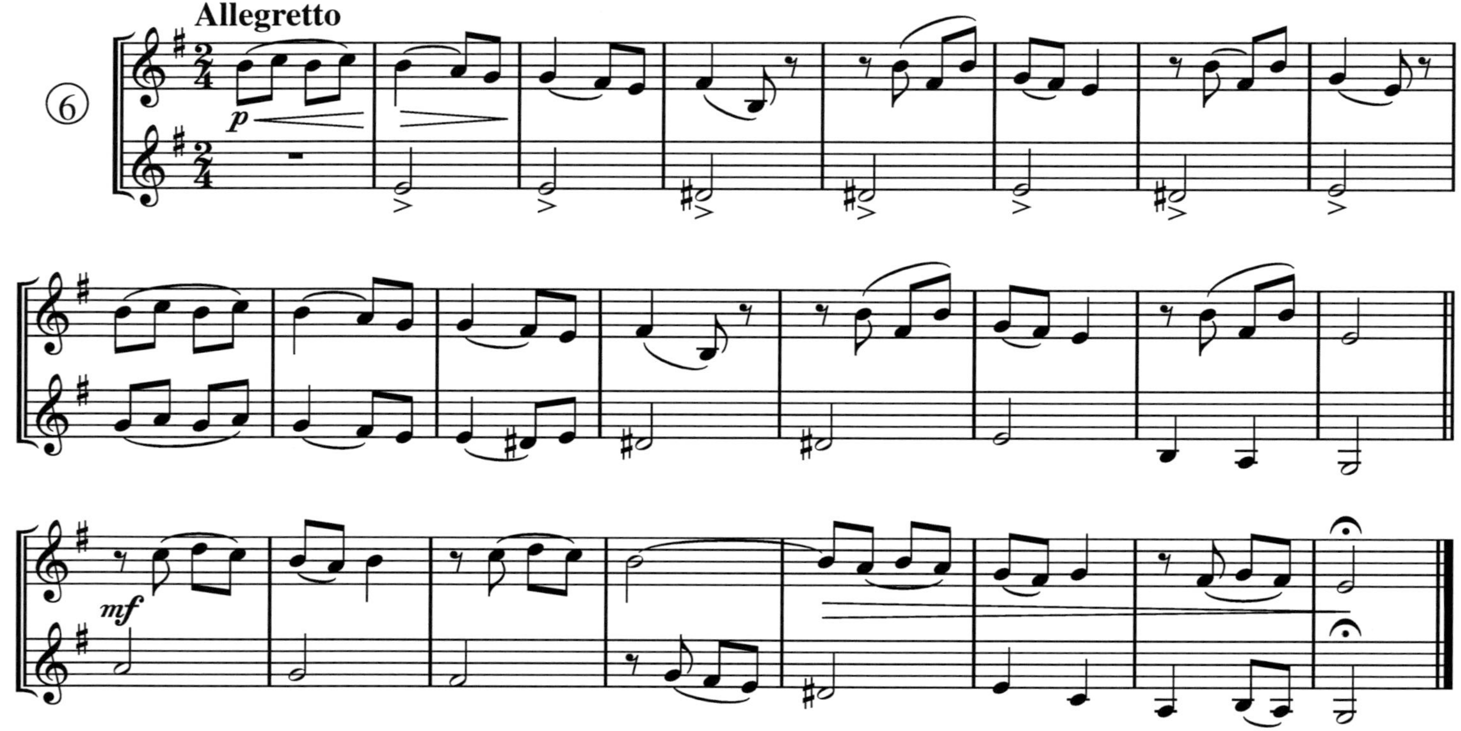

Spanish Royal March

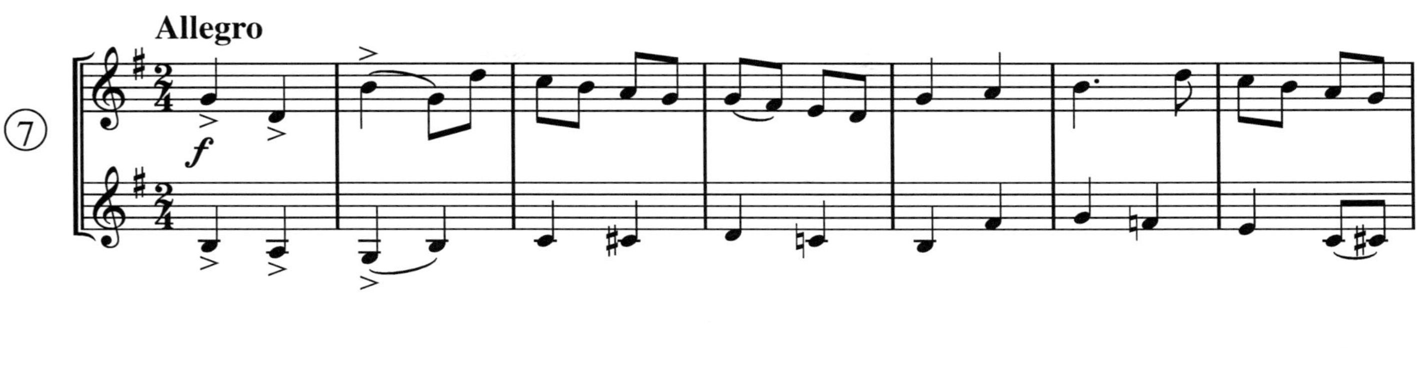

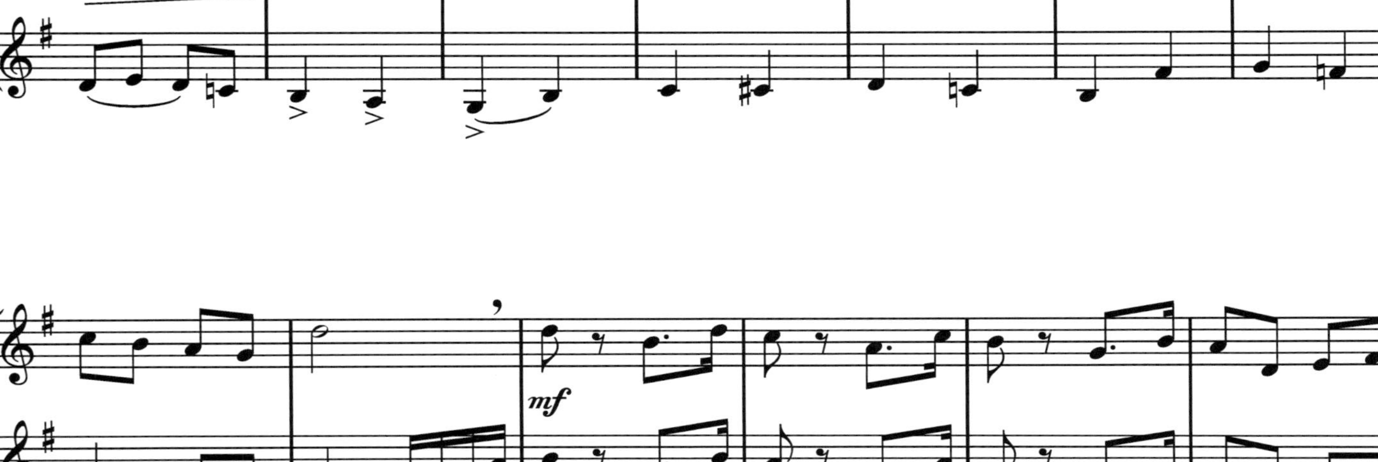

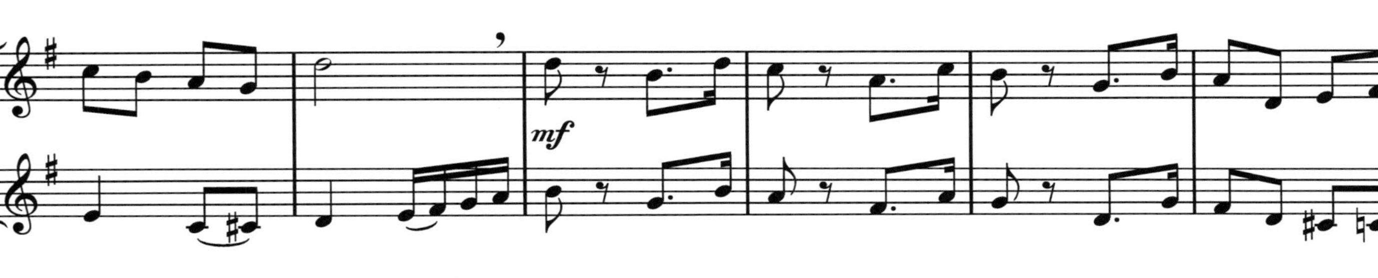

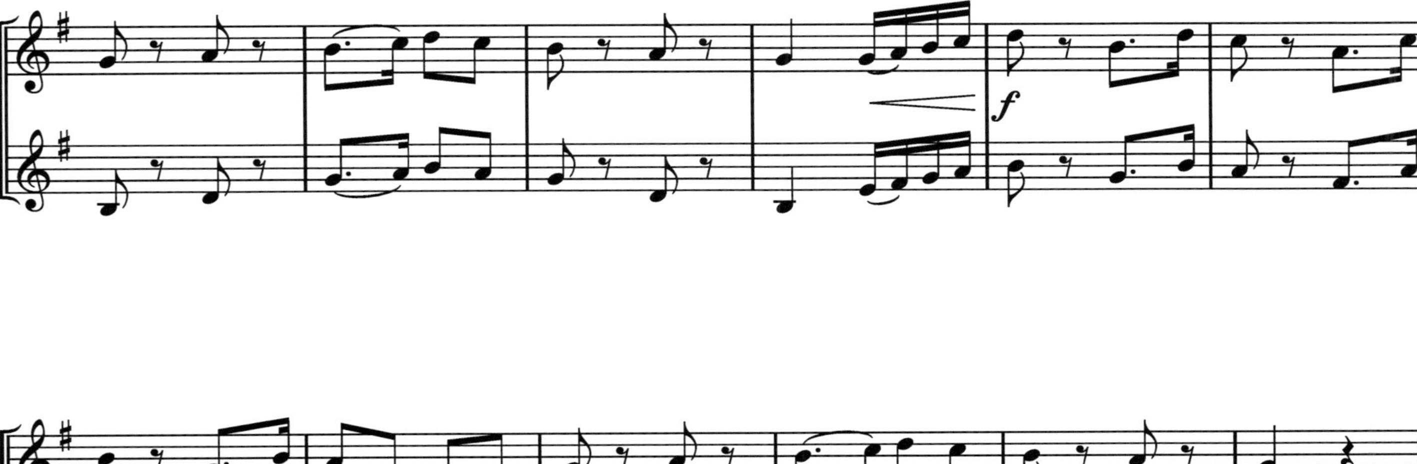

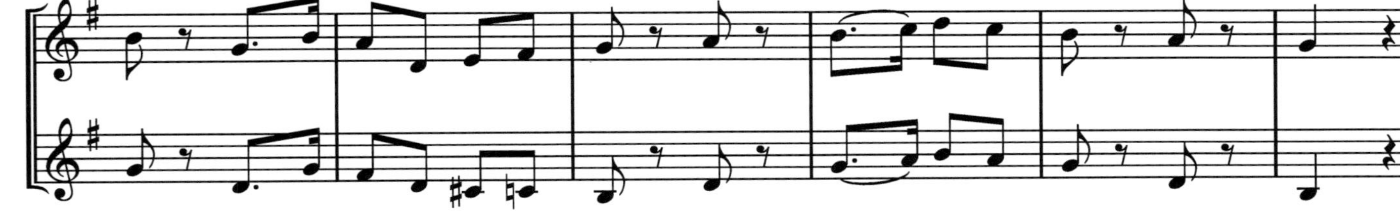

Bivouac Song

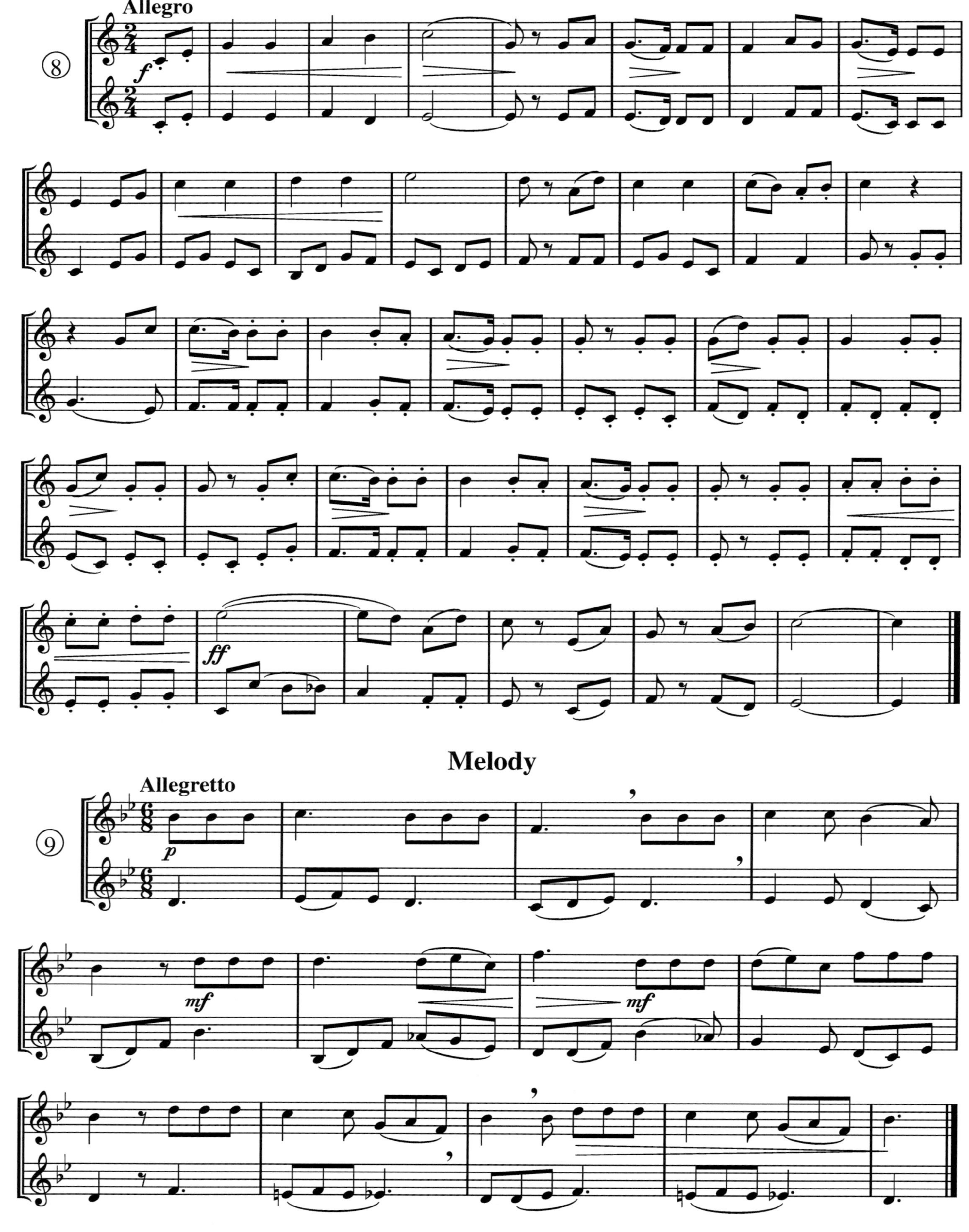

Melody

Two Great Characteristic Studies

correlates to No. 1, page 350 in *Complete Conservatory Method*

Number 1

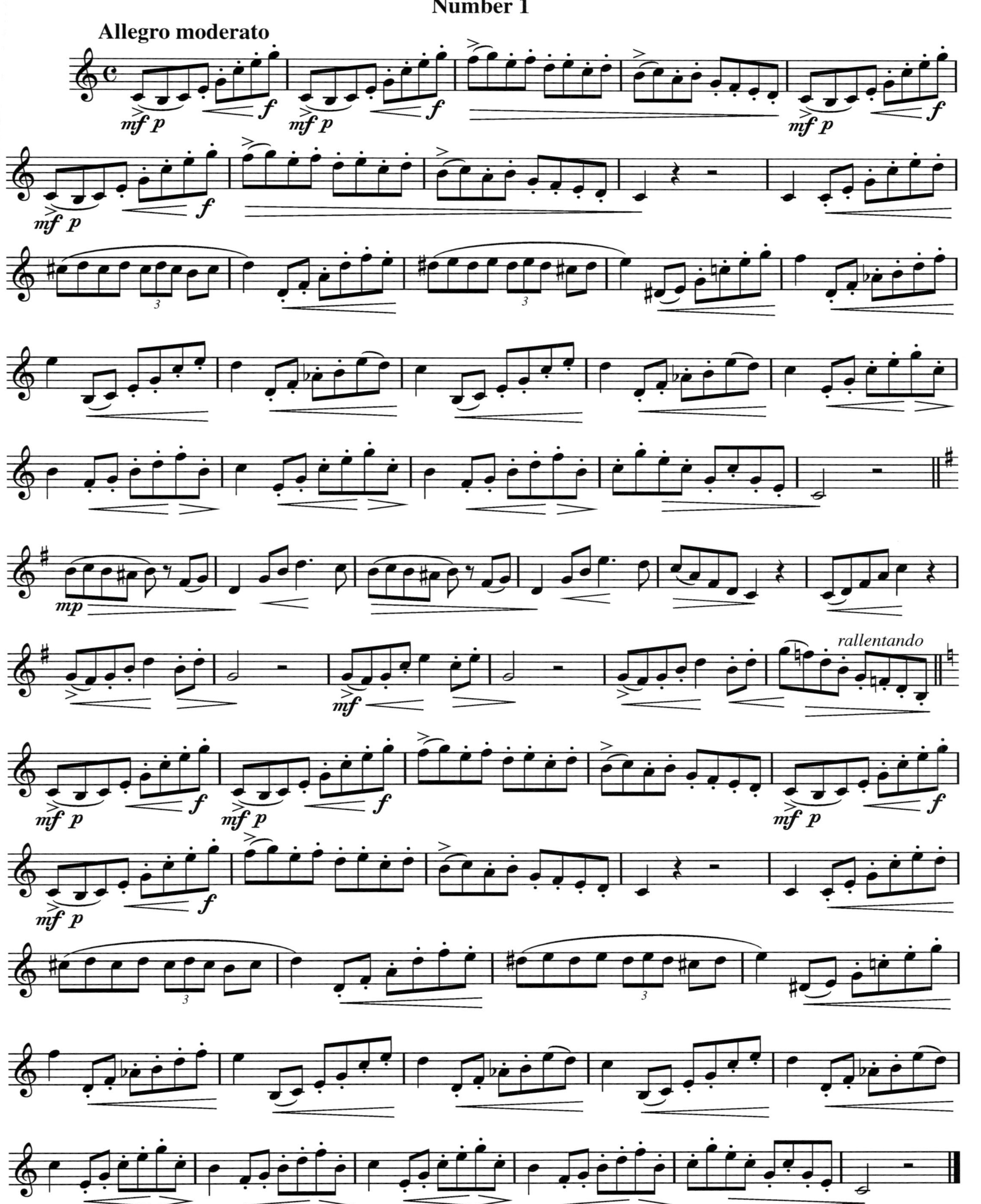

correlates to No. 8, page 364 in *Complete Conservatory Method*

Number 8

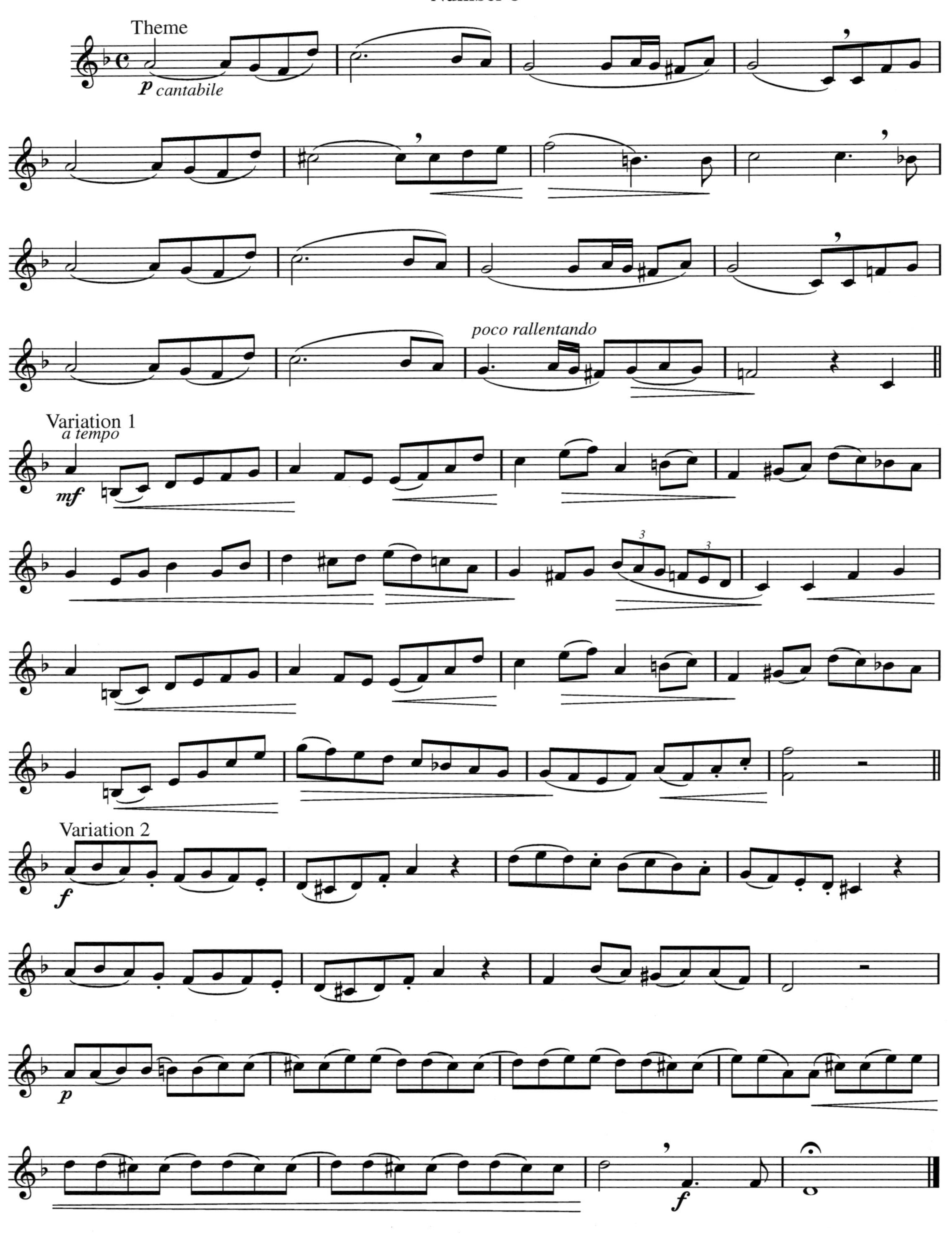